THE COMPLETE GUIDE TO SCHNOODLES

Vanessa Richie

Publication Data

Schnoodles

The Complete Guide to Schnoodles – First edition.

Summary: "Successfully raising a Schnoodle Dog from puppy to old age" – Provided by publisher.

ISBN: 978-1-952069-85-7

[1. Schnoodles – Non-Fiction] I. Title.

Design by Sorin Rădulescu

First paperback edition, 2020

TABLE OF CONTENTS

CHAPTER 10

Socialization

CHAPTER 11

Training Your Schnoodle

CHAPTER 12

Nutrition

CHAPTER 15

General Health Issues: Allergies, Parasites, and Vaccinations

CHAPTER 16

Genetic Health Concerns Common to the Schnoodle

INTRODUCTION

The Schnoodle is a designer breed of dog, which means they are intentionally bred from two different breeds – in this case, a Schnauzer and a Poodle. These are two extremely different breeds, but they are both friendly and loving. Both breeds can be a bit headstrong, so you will need to prepare to be firm and consistent with your Schnoodle. Schnoodles are smart, and they love playing and being active. Like all dogs, they need both physical and mental exercise. If you like to train dogs, this breed picks up tricks and commands very quickly!

As a designer breed, Schnoodles vary in appearance, including the color and type of their coat. As with most Poodle mixes, one of the biggest attractions of a Schnoodle puppy is the idea that they will likely be hypoallergenic - thanks to their Poodle parent. Equally attractive is that adorable, fluffy, playful dog-look that makes people choose the Schnoodle as a pet!

While you can find Schnoodles in many sizes (both parent breeds come in three different sizes), the majority of breeders focus on smaller to medium-sized dogs. Due to this range in sizes, if you adopt from a breeder, you will need to ask about the dog's parents. Knowing how big your adult Schnoodle will grow affects everything from how much the dog will eat to how much exercise it will need. This information will also help calculate the odds of your dog developing different ailments.

You will also find a wide range of personalities when comparing the Poodle to the Schnauzer. They both love their families, which is a nice guarantee! Poodles tend to be intelligent, friendly, and a bit willful while Schnauzers are inclined to be energetic, intelligent, alert, and slightly wary of others. The former is known for being dignified while the latter is apt to be more athletic. Both breeds can be very obedient, but they also require a reason to listen to you before they willingly follow your commands. Luckily, neither breed is particularly difficult to train. Socialization tends to be easy, but you will need to make sure to begin early as Schnauzers can be a bit aloof and wary of strangers and other dogs. Smaller Poodles can also be problematic when around people and other dogs, so you will need to socialize your Schnoodle right from the beginning.

The Schnoodle is a fantastic breed for families and people who like to stay active. They are inclined to be loving and affectionate dogs, which makes for a reliable and happy companion!

CHAPTER 1
Breed History And Characteristics Of The Schnoodle

When the Schnoodle was first bred during the 1980s, different Poodle breeds were becoming extremely popular because they were hypoallergenic. The breed is too new to be recognized by any of the major dog organizations, such as the American Kennel Club. This also means there is no standard for their appearance or their temperament. Over time this may change, but for now, adopting a Schnoodle means you are getting a bit of a wildcard in terms of size, looks, and temperament. There are some similar personality traits between the two breeds; still, the two parent breeds are distinctly different.

Although Schnoodles may have a brief history, both of their parent breeds have been around for a long time. To understand the Schnoodle breed more clearly, you have to understand the history of the parent breeds. The history of both breeds has one thing in common – they were originally bred in Germany to be working dogs.

Schnauzer

The Standard Schnauzer was the first type of dog to be bred increasingly smaller over time. Schnauzers have a longer history than other breeds and were known as Pinschers for quite some time. They were an important part of the home because they were instrumental in working around the farm, particularly with tending the livestock. When their owners were going to the market, the dogs joined them to protect them. Over time, they were bred to be smaller so they could more easily catch rodents and pests around the farm. Their wiry coats were ideal for this life because their coats didn't require much attention or grooming.

During the 1800s, Standard Schnauzers were bred with several other dog breeds to give them their distinctive look and a wider range in size. This time, breeding was due to a desire to change the dogs' look than for the purpose of acquiring specific abilities. The two primary breeds that were used were the Wolf Spitz and the black German Poodle; this mix is what gives today's Schnauzers their distinctive salt-and-pepper coat.

Up to this point, the Standard Schnauzer was still a fairly decent size – it was not a small dog! This changed, however, as people no longer needed

Photo Courtesy
of Dara Davis

Photo Courtesy
of Lynn Gotsis

large dogs for work on the farm. Instead, they wanted smaller dogs to accommodate their changing lifestyles which had moved indoors.

Shortly after, people decided they wanted bigger versions of this smaller dog, so they started breeding the biggest versions of the parent breeds, resulting in the Giant Schnauzer. This new breed was shown at a German exhibition for the first time during the 1870s, and from the description, they were similar to the modern-day Standard Schnauzer. This is noteworthy because breeds tend to look quite different over the span of 100 years, yet this breed has largely looked the same for far longer. People began to call them Schnauzers because of their very square snouts. In German, a dog's muzzle is called die Schnauze. This physical characteristic tends to be one of the first things people notice about this dog.

Different sizes of the breed exhibit different personality traits, but all sizes are known to be intelligent and protective of their homes; they are also energetic and playful, particularly miniature Schnauzers. Schnoodles tend to be good with other dogs, but their long history of chasing creatures has given them an incredibly high prey drive. This is why people are told to be careful when bringing Schnauzers into a home with small pets, such as cats and rodents. They are not the best lapdogs because they are too active; however, they do well in homes with active owners who want an adventurous companion.

Poodles

The Poodle is descended from an Asian canine breed and is one of the oldest pure breeds in existence. Some experts believe they arrived with the Goths from western Asia and were used as hunting companions. The unique curls to their coats give away their ties to the Asian breeds, and they are likely related to many curly-haired European water dogs.

From the beginning, Poodles were working dogs. The German tribes used them as hunting dogs; in fact, there are people in Europe who still insist this breed accompany them on hunting trips. In France, they became popular companions for duck hunters because of the way their fur repelled water. Over time, Poodles became working dogs in other professions, such as

FUN FACT
Giant Schnoodles

Schnoodles come in a variety of colors, but did you know that they also come in different sizes? The Giant Schnoodle is the result of a Giant Schnauzer and a Standard Poodle and has the same loveable characteristics as its regular-sized counterpart!

the military, although their temperament did not make them nearly as effective as some of the other popular guard dogs of today. In addition to all of these talents, they really thrived as circus performers and entertainers.

Like the Schnauzer, Poodles are intelligent and loving. They have an easygoing personality and enjoy engaging with their owners in entertaining tricks and games. There is a logical reason why this breed has been so incredibly popular for so long – it is extremely versatile. While no dog is fully hypoallergenic, most people with allergies can live with Poodles without suffering any reactions. All of this, coupled with how affectionate they can be, make Poodles a fantastic choice for virtually any home!

With the Poodle parent, having such a long and close history living with humans, the Schnoodle is certain to be easily integrated into your family. Even if your pup gets some of the stubbornness or the wariness of the breed, your newest family member will still exhibit loads of great qualities from both sides!

A Brief History Of The Schnoodle

"Schnoodles are known for their intelligence and loyalty. Two highly intelligent dog breeds mixed together makes the Schnoodle an amazingly smart dog."

ANGELA DENNY
Angela's Schnoodles

The Schnoodle breed is still relatively new to the dog community. People began intentionally breeding Schnoodles in Minnesota in the 1980s. There are more Schnoodle pups born from Schnoodle parents than many other mixed breeds because Schnoodles have been around for about four decades. Today, the Schnoodle has no notable ancestors, and they are not eligible for registration, so they cannot be recognized as a pedigree even if both parents are purebred dogs.

One of the main reasons the Schnoodle is so popular is due to the breed's hypoallergenic properties and the boom of "Doodle" breeds. While the term hypoallergenic isn't exactly what people think it is (Chapter 2) and there is no guarantee that a mixed breed will be hypoallergenic, the hope

Photo Courtesy of Erin Shafto

that doodle mixes will cause less problems is what has made them so popular. Besides that, this dog is a combination of two dogs that have been around for centuries and are known for their positive qualities.

There are three types of Schnoodles: There is the Standard Schnoodle that is a cross between a Standard Schnauzer and a Standard Poodle. The Miniature Schnoodle is a cross between a Miniature Schnauzer and a Miniature Poodle. The largest Schnoodle is typically a cross between the Giant Schnauzer and Standard Poodle. These are the usual parent combinations, but breeders sometimes mix the sizes. So, if you buy from a breeder, you will need to ask about the size of the parents so you have a rough idea of how large your Schnoodle puppy will eventually grow.

A Quick Word About Designer Dogs

While many designer dogs are bred for looks alone, the American Kennel Club advocates for pure breeds with longer histories and established temperaments, particularly those breeds that have declined in numbers, such as Otterhounds. The AKC's argument is that it is unnecessary for people to intentionally create a new breed of dog because many established breeds have the same sought-after traits through normal selective breeding. It is easier to predict the potential risks and problems of a single breed of dog than it is to establish a consistent new breed by crossing two different varieties of dog.

The American Kennel Club's concern is certainly legitimate, particularly when considering puppy mills that only seek a profit from designer-dog trends. As will be covered in a later chapter, looking into the parents' health and history is just as important for designer dogs as it is for purebred dogs. You should find a breeder who knows the parents well, has experienced their personalities, and who takes good care of both. Learning their parentage gives you an accurate idea of what your puppy's temperament and health will be.

When purchasing a designer dog, you also want to find a breeder who loves dogs and knows how to breed them correctly; not someone who is simply trying to make a lot of money from the latest trend. Owning a designer dog comes with enough variables without adding problems created by uncaring breeders. As long as you research your breeder, your Schnoodle can be an incredible companion that is cuddly and loving!

Schnoodles are not recognized by most large canine clubs, but with their high activity levels, they tend to be good in many different arenas. If interested, you can register your dog for certain performance training activities, such as agility and flyball competition.

CHAPTER 2
Schnoodle Attributes And Temperament

"I have found over the past nine years of breeding Schnoodles that they are a very adaptable breed who are able to go into a variety of living situations. I have Schnoodle families living from the Southernmost tip of Florida all the way to Canada. Some are in apartments, others in huge 3,000 acre farms. Some are family pets and others service dogs. And in the service dogs, the owners range from small children to older adults and they do all different kinds of service! They are a VERY adaptable breed indeed!"

CATHERINE WILSON
Oodles of Schnoodles

Schnoodles haven't gained the same level of attention as "Doodle" breeds, but that doesn't mean they aren't a fantastic addition to the home. They have a Poodle's desire to make their people happy but with the active nature of a Schnauzer. They also seem to be sturdier than most Poodles because of their Schnauzer parent. They love being the center of attention, and with this kind of temperament, it doesn't take long for the Schnoodle to become an important member of your family. Give your Schnoodle the right training and keep him active, and he will be a marvelous companion!

Predicting Appearance

Schnoodles have so many different looks you can actually mistake some of them for a different breed entirely! They are too new to have a set standard, and to some people, their differences are part of their charm. Spending a few minutes checking out Schnoodle images online will show you just how diverse the breed can be. If you decide to adopt a puppy, you will find that even in the same litter, the puppies are all incredibly unique. What is consistent in the breed is its wonderful temperament. Schnoodle puppies are typically loving, little balls of energy that will want to be by your side wherever you go!

Schnauzer Appearance

Easily the most distinctive feature of a Schnauzer is a muzzle with a square look and a long mustache. They are a terrier breed, so they have a very distinctive terrier appearance, including the shape of their body and head. They are primarily grey, white, and black, and they have been described as having a salt-and-pepper or black and silver look. It is a striking look, especially with their long mustaches and their wiry coats!

On those rectangular-looking heads are a set of noticeable eyebrows that have been called Einstein eyebrows, and they can grow to surprising lengths if not trimmed regularly. A Schnauzer's ears flop over in nearly perfect triangles, giving them a friendly appearance in addition to those intelligent eyes and impressive eyebrows. Their size varies:

*Photo Courtesy
of Michelle Padgett*

- Giant Schnauzers weigh between 65 and 90 pounds, and their height ranges from 23 to 27 inches.
- Standard Schnauzers weigh between 35 and 45 pounds, and their height ranges from 17 to 20 inches.
- Miniature Schnauzers are the smallest, weighing between 13 and 15 pounds and ranging from 12 to 14 inches in height.

They have a fairly long, whip-like tail and a barrel chest which holds their large lungs, and their front legs look fairly short, particularly compared to their long back legs. However, it can be hard to focus on a Schnauzer's powerful legs because people ultimately focus on that fuzzy coat instead of the legs underneath all that fur. They have a very sturdy frame, and their large chest doesn't taper off nearly as fast as other breeds, which gives them more of a rectangular body shape (especially compared to the Poodle).

Poodle Appearance

One of the most popular dog breeds, people can usually identify a Poodle on sight, regardless of the Poodle's size. They are one of the most easily recognizable dogs in the world! It's their incredible coat, which is quite easy to style, that draws peoples' attention. Their curly coats come in a variety of colors:

- Apricot (rare)
- Black
- Blue
- Brown
- Cream (rare)
- Gray
- Red
- Silver
- White

Unlike the Schnauzer, the Poodle's coat is soft, especially on their ears. They have long, narrow noses, long floppy ears, and a mop of fur on their heads. Poodles are similar in size to the Schnauzer:

- Standard Poodles weigh between 45 and 70 pounds, and their height ranges from 15 to 22 inches.
- Miniature Poodles weigh between 15 and 18 pounds and are about 15 inches tall.
- Toy Poodles are the smallest, weighing between 6 and 9 pounds, and their height is approximately 10 inches tall.

With a large chest and graceful-looking form, you can see the similarities between the two breeds. A Poodle's tail is usually a bit shorter than the

Photo Courtesy
of Dan Vasili

Schnauzer's tail, and their fur makes them look a lot like a toy; this is true for all three Poodle sizes. Compared to the Schnauzer, the Poodle is also thinner and has a more elegant look.

Different Schnoodle Sizes

Schnoodles can be as small as a Toy Poodle or as large as a Giant Schnauzer depending on the size of their parents. This is why it is incredibly

Photo Courtesy
of Kally-Anna Clinton

important to know the size of your dog's parents when you decide to own a puppy. Your Schnoodle's size will be even less predictable if he is a second generation Schnoodle because these puppies can be as small or as large as any one of their four grandparents. There are four identifiable sizes for the Schnoodle based on the varied sizes of the two initial breeds and the size of the parents:

- Giant Schnoodles weigh between 65 and 85 pounds, and their height ranges from 24 to 28 inches. Usually one parent is a Giant Schnauzer and the other is a Standard Poodle.
- Standard Schnoodles weigh between 20 and 75 pounds, and their height ranges from 16 to 26 inches. (This does overlap with the Giant Schnoodle.) The parents are usually a Standard Schnauzer and Standard Poodle.
- Miniature Schnoodles weigh between 14 and 20 pounds, and their height ranges from 12 to 16 inches. The parents of this Schnoodle are the Miniature Schnauzer and Miniature Poodle.
- Toy Schnoodles are the smallest, ranging between 6 and 14 pounds and between 8 to 12 inches tall. The parents are a Miniature Schnauzer and a Toy Poodle.

Chapter 4 provides more details about planning a budget based on your dog's size. Initially, you won't need to buy large cages, food, or collars, but you should at least budget for a larger dog - just in case.

A Family Dog – The Likely Temperaments Of The Schnoodle

"Schnoodles are very friendly dogs that love everyone they meet. This breed is perfect for anyone who is looking for a very obedient, loving, intelligent, loyal and fluffy friend. Schnoodles are very laid-back, so if you want to just lay around the house they are a good fit, but they also love to go for walks and runs."

ANGELA DENNY
Angela's Schnoodles

While you can't completely predict your dog's temperament, you can be prepared for some differences.

Keep in mind that temperament and behavior are not the same. You can guide your dog into exhibiting acceptable behavior through proper training (Chapters 9 and 11) and socialization (Chapter 10). His temperament, however, is a result of his breeding.

Schnauzer Temperament

Schnauzers of all sizes are known for their energy levels. In Miniature Schnauzers, this can translate to more barking, while in larger Schnauzers, it might manifest as a need for longer walks. These dogs are notorious for being playful, which can make them perfect for children, especially older ones, because Schnauzers can easily keep up with your child's activity level.

They can also be stubborn, so early training is essential! Their desire to stay busy combined with their intelligence make them an ideal candidate for agility training. Since they have a long history of protecting people, they also make great watchdogs.

Schnauzers usually choose one person, over the rest of the family, to whom they become attached. They will love their "family pack" as a whole, but they tend to treat one person as a favorite creature (or alpha) since they crave structure. In the wild, dog packs have a dog that is in charge, so there is more dedication to the person in charge because that person is the one who makes the decisions.

Poodle Temperament

Though not quite as spirited as the Schnauzer, Poodles do have plenty of energy! They are also known for being intelligent, and coupled with their

Photo Courtesy of Lisa Schmidt

playful nature, this can result in trouble on a regular basis! Poodles don't like to be left alone, so many suffer from separation anxiety. However, when people are home, this breed is incredibly well-behaved and is one of the most obedient dog breeds.

Predicting The Schnoodle Temperament

Your Schnoodle could end up with any of the above personality traits, so you need to plan for all of them. The Schnoodle is known for being energetic and playful, and it is also a safe bet your dog will be intelligent; so, training beyond the basics is a possibility if you also want to teach your dog tricks.

Schnoodles are affection- ate with their people but can be

wary of strangers. They are more likely to defend their family members than other Poodle mixes because of the Schnauzer's long history of being protective. Luckily, Schnoodles are not as stubborn or as hyper as a Schnauzer!

Smaller Schnoodles may be prolific diggers or barkers. (Larger versions are less likely to develop these traits, but you should still plan for it...just in case.) Smaller dogs can be quite a handful with their digging and high energy level, but it is easier to get this out of their system because of their size. A Giant Schnauzer can be a wildcard due to their high-energy levels and their feistiness.

SCHNOODLES IN BOOKS
Schnoodle and Sam

Schnoodle and Sam is a delightfully illustrated book by Canadian-American cartoonist Eric Gurney, chronicling the friendship between a Schnoodle and a cat named Sam. Published in 1981, this picture book came out just one year after Schnoodles were first created.

Potentially Hypoallergenic

Given their wiry fur and hypoallergenic Poodle parentage, some people assume Schnauzers are hypoallergenic, too. The reality is that it is more about what kind of dander a dog produces. If you are more allergic to a particular type of dander, you will have an allergic reaction regardless of how others react. Since Schnoodles are not purebred dogs, there is no way to know if you will be allergic to your dog's shedding skin cells. That is simply something you learn over time.

Maybe Too Much For Beginners

Poodles are on most dog organization lists, including the American Kennel Club, as the best choice for first-time pet owners. Still, Schnauzers are a bit more difficult to handle – they are a great breed but are not recommended for people with no experience as a dog owner. A Poodle's calm character trait might be prominent in your Schnoodle, but there is never a guarantee. Instead of taking a risk, starting as a Poodle owner - or another recommended breed of dog with a calm temperament – might be the best decision for you. Once you have a bit of experience – especially with training your dog – you can bring one of these amazing Schnoodle breeds into your home!

CHAPTER 3
Finding Your Schnoodle

D eciding a Schnoodle is the right dog for you is only the first step in the exciting journey of adopting your next family member. The hunt for the perfect partner may take a while and depends on whether you decide to buy a puppy or to rescue an adult.

Bringing Home An Adult Schnoodle

With a breed like the Schnoodle, you need to be careful about adopting an adult; if the dog is not properly trained, life can turn into a real struggle. Adopting an older Schnoodle could require a lot of work so knowing the dog's history is incredibly important in order to prepare for the dog's behavior.

Schnoodles can be stubborn and an adult might also be a bit more wary, especially if it hasn't been socialized or was previously treated poorly. Unless the dog's history with children is a positive one, you should not adopt an adult if you have young children in your home. Similarly, you should be careful about adopting a Schnoodle if you have other pets at home.

On the positive side, older dogs can give you more immediate gratification. You don't have to go through the sleepless nights that come with a new puppy. The odds are also probable that you aren't going to be starting from scratch with housetraining.

Additionally, adult dogs are awake during the day more than puppies, and while it may take your dog a bit longer to warm up to you, you can bond much faster with an adult.

CELEBRITY SCHNOODLES

Pippa the Schnoodle Cyclist ★★★★★

Pippa the Schnoodle was adopted when she was two or three years old from the Humane Society of the Southeast in Newnan, Georgia, by Todd Steigerwalt. Right away, Steigerwalt, a lifelong cyclist and triathlete, purchased a chest harness for Pippa and began taking her along on his bike rides. Eventually, the harness was replaced by their current setup, a backpack and goggles.

The duo ride together up to three times per week! You can follow Pippa's adventures on her personal Instagram (@ pippaofpiedmont)

Photo Courtesy
of Barrie and Danielle Gotch
from Waggies Wonderdogs

Finally, one of the biggest benefits of acquiring an adult dog is that they are already their full size. There is no need for guessing how big your dog will grow, and that makes it far easier to purchase the appropriate-sized gear and dog supplies right from the start.

The following is a list of questions to consider when adopting an adult Schnoodle:

- **Can you properly dog-proof your home before the dog arrives?**

  You can't simply bring a dog into your home, whether an adult or a puppy, and let him run around unchecked. To be sure he learns the rules of the house before roaming freely, you will need to have a safe, dedicated space for your new dog. (Details of how to dog-proof your home are discussed in Chapter 5.)

- **Do you have pets who will be affected by a new dog?**

  Schnoodles are more aggressive toward other dogs and animals than they are toward people. If the dog's history with other pets is not known, it is best not to select that particular adult dog unless you can ensure a slow, careful introduction to your current family pets. This introduction should take place over the first couple of months. Introducing them in neutral territory will show you what to expect when your Schnoodle and your current dogs are together on a permanent basis. Even if they appear to be compatible, you still need to keep them apart for longer than you would with most breeds. This will ensure your new Schnoodle understands that other dogs are part of the pack and are not a threat to him.

  You will need to be aware of how your other dog(s) reacts as well. Schnoodles are very bossy, so if you already have an alpha dog, it may be difficult for them to get along. Even if your current dog is very friendly, you will still want to be careful when introducing the two and allowing them to interact in your home.

- **What is the dog's health history?**

  A complete health record for a rescue Schnoodle may not be available, but it is likely you will find a dog that has already been spayed or neutered, as well as chipped. Unless you adopt a Schnoodle with health issues, which should be disclosed by the rescue organization if known, rescues tend to be less costly than puppies at their first vet visit. In other words, for the first few years, your Schnoodle's health care visits should not be too expensive.

Bringing Home A Schnoodle Puppy

Puppies are a major time investment, and a dog as intelligent and stubborn as the Schnoodle will make some aspects of raising a puppy that much harder. How much time can you devote to a puppy's care? Will you be able to deal with an excitable puppy that has everything to learn?

A puppy will be a better fit if you put in dedicated time for training and socializing before the dog becomes set in his ways. If you have other pets at home, a puppy is definitely a better choice than an adult because he is young and can be trained to follow YOUR rules. (The exception would be if you find an adult that is already well-socialized.)

The following should be considered when determining whether or not a Schnoodle puppy is a good fit for your home:

- **How much time do you have available for training and socialization?**

  One of the biggest considerations is how much time you are willing to invest in your new puppy. All puppies are a lot of work, starting with the moment the puppy enters your care. While the Schnoodle's temperament is largely predictable, how you train and socialize your puppy will affect every aspect of the dog's adult life. Training and socializing can take up a large chunk of time in the beginning, but both are absolutely essential for raising a healthy Schnoodle.

- **Are you able to show firmness and consistency when training such an adorable puppy?**

  From the very beginning, you have to establish yourself and your family as the ones in charge; your Schnoodle must understand his place in the family hierarchy. You will need to be patient and consistent with your training, no matter how frustrated you become or how cute those puppy eyes appear. All intelligent dogs have a streak of stubbornness!

- **Do you have the time, energy, and budget to puppy-proof your home?**

  The preparation of your home for your puppy's arrival begins long before he first sets foot in your house. Puppy-proofing your home is as time consuming as child-proofing your home. If you do not have the time for this, then you should consider getting an adult dog instead of a puppy. (Details of how-to puppy-proof your home are discussed in Chapter 5.)

  What most people love about adopting a puppy is that they will spend more time with a puppy than with an adult dog since they still have their whole lives ahead of them. You will receive records about the puppy and the puppy's parents, which will make it easier to identify any prob-

Photo Courtesy
of Jennifer Henry-Smith

lems your Schnoodle might experience in the future. This makes it considerably easier to keep your puppy healthy and to spot potential issues before they become major problems.

Some people find it easier to bond with puppies than with adult dogs. A young puppy may be nervous in a new home, but most adjust quickly because they are predisposed to enjoying the company of those around them.

A Word Of Advice

We strongly recommend avoiding pet stores when searching for the perfect Schnoodle. Beware of puppy mills and pet stores that might not properly breed or care for their dogs. Many problems can arise at the beginning of a puppy's life from inappropriate conditions and treatment. To ensure you find a healthy puppy to be your loving companion for as long as possible, you must find a reputable breeder who cares about his dogs. Do your research before purchasing! With a Schnoodle's life span ranging from ten to fifteen years, you will want to have as much protection as possible against genetic ailments; this means finding a breeder who always puts his puppies' health first.

Unlike purebred dogs, potential genetic problems for the Schnoodle come from two different breeds; luckily, both breeds are fairly well-documented when it comes to health concerns. (Details are discussed in Chapter 16.) You should learn the medical history of the puppy's parents to ensure your puppy has the best chance of living a healthy, happy life. However, it is also important to know what diseases are common to both of the parent breeds even if they are not currently present.

Rescuing A Schnoodle

Since this is a new breed, there are few Schnoodle-specific rescue organizations around the country. However, if you are considering rescuing a Schnoodle, you can always start with your local organizations that are not breed-specific. Schnoodle Rescue, a website that lists rescue sites for all breeds, is a wonderful place to start because it connects with different regions of the US.

Instead of searching rescue organizations, you might want to rescue a Schnoodle from a breeder. They will have a better understanding of the dog and its personality, and they will be able to answer any future questions you might have.

> **Keep in mind the following questions whether you adopt a Schnoodle from an organization or from a breeder:**
> - What is the reason the dog was surrendered?
> - Did the dog have any health issues when he arrived?
> - Do they know how the dog was treated by the previous family?
> - (What kind of training was he given, was he mistreated, and was he socialized?)
> - How many homes has the dog experienced?
> - What kind of veterinarian care did the dog receive? Are there records that confirm this?
> - Will the dog require extra medical attention based on known or suspected problems?
> - Is the dog housetrained?
> - How well does the dog react to strangers while walking in unfamiliar areas?
> - Does the dog have good eating habits, or does he tend to be more aggressive when eating?
> - How does the dog react to children and to other dogs and pets?
> - Does he have any known allergies?
> - Does the dog have any known dietary restrictions?
> - If there are problems with the dog after adoption, will the organization take him back?

Rescue groups should have at least a basic understanding of how the Schnoodle interacts with other dogs.

Choosing A Breeder

Finding a responsible breeder is the best thing you can do for your puppy because good breeders work only with healthy Schnoodle parents, which reduces the odds of serious health issues.

Always take the time to do your research before moving forward. You can start with breeders in surrounding areas in your state, or you can start researching sites that are strictly dedicated to the breed. Although breeders for Schnoodles are largely reputable, you also might run across an individual who is more interested in making a lot of money than in caring for their dogs. Beware!

The goal is to locate breeders who are willing to answer ALL of your questions patiently and thoroughly. They should show as much love for

Photo Courtesy
of Regan Yougberg

their Schnoodles as they expect you to show for your new puppy; their goal should be to locate good homes for all of their animals.

It is a particularly good sign if you find a breeder who posts pictures and information about the dog's parents, progress of the mother's pregnancy, and descriptions of all vet visits. The best breeders will also stay in contact with you and answer any questions that might arise after you take the puppy home.

Unfortunately for you, these are also the breeders who are likely to have waiting lists. Taking an active interest in what happens to the puppies in their new home shows that they care a great deal about each individual dog.

You also want to find a breeder who is willing to talk about problems that might develop with your Schnoodle. Good breeders will ensure the adopting family is capable of properly socializing and training their Schnoodle since both of these activities are essential as a puppy matures.

It is likely that your conversation with each breeder will last about an hour. If a breeder does not have time to talk when you call and isn't willing to call you back - cross them off your list! Also, after you have talked with each possible breeder, take the time to compare their answers to your questions and make sure you take careful notes during every interview.

The following are some questions to consider when researching breeders:

- Ask if you can visit in person. The answer should always be yes, and if it isn't, you don't need to ask anything further. Thank the breeder and hang up. Even if the breeder is located in a different state, they should always allow you to visit their facility.

- Ask about the required health tests and certifications they have for their puppies. (These points are detailed further in the next section so make sure to check off the available tests and certifications – with every breeder.) If they don't have all of the tests and certifications, remove the breeder from your list of considerations.

- Make sure the breeder takes care of the initial health requirements, particularly shots, for each puppy – from the first few weeks of birth through the dog's early months. Puppies require certain procedures before they leave their mother in order to ensure they are healthy. Vaccinations and worming typically start around six weeks of age and should be continued every three weeks. By the time your puppy is old enough to come home, he should be well into the first phase of these procedures or completely finished with these important health care needs.

- Ask if the puppy is required to be spayed or neutered before reaching a certain age. Typically, these procedures are completed with the puppy's best interest in mind.

- Question whether or not the breeder is part of a Schnoodle organization or group.

- Ask about the first phases of your puppy's life, such as how the breeder will care for the puppy prior to going home with you. They should be able to provide a lot of details, and they should not sound irritated by your questioning. They should also explain what training your puppy will received prior to leaving the facility. It is also possible the breeder might start housetraining your puppy. If so, ask about the puppy's progress so you know where to pick up training once your Schnoodle reaches your home.

- The breeder should give good advice about raising your Schnoodle puppy. They should be more than happy to help guide you in doing what is best for your dog because they should want their puppies to live happy, healthy lives. You should also be able to rely on any recommendations your breeder makes about taking your puppy home, particularly about those first days with the puppy in your home.

- Ask how many varieties of dogs the breeder manages in one year and how many sets of parents he owns. Puppies can take a lot of time and attention when first born, and the mother should have some downtime between pregnancies before producing another litter. Learn about the breeder's standard operations to be sure they take care of the parents and treat them like valuable family members - not strictly as a way to make money.

- Ask about aggression in the puppy's parents and find out if there are other dogs in the breeder's home. While a puppy's temperament is more malleable than an adult, some exposure to other breeds might make it easier when integrating them into a home that already has dogs.

Contracts And Guarantees

Breeder contracts and guarantees are meant to protect the puppies as much as they are meant to protect you. If a breeder has a contract that must be signed, make sure you read through it completely and are willing to meet all of the requirements prior to signing. Contracts tend to be fairly easy to understand and to comply with, but you should be aware of all the facts before you agree to anything. Signing the contract indicates you are serious about committing to giving your puppy the best care possible and to meeting the minimum care requirements set forth by the breeder.

A contract may also state the breeder will retain the puppy's original registration papers although you will receive a copy of the papers, too.

If a family does not meet all requirements as stated in the contract, it is the breeder's responsibility to remove that puppy from the family. These are the dogs some breeders offer for adoption.

A guarantee states the kind of health conditions the breeder's puppy is to receive once it leaves the breeder's facility. This typically includes details about the dog's current health and the recommendations for the next steps in the puppy's health care. Guarantees may also provide veterinary schedules to ensure that the health care started by the breeder is continued by the new puppy parent. In the event that a major health concern surfaces, the puppy will be returned to the breeder.

The contract will also explain what is not covered by the guarantee. A guarantee tends to be quite long (sometimes longer than the contract), and you should also read it thoroughly before the signing.

Schnoodle contracts usually include a requirement that the dog be spayed or neutered once it reaches maturity (typically six months). The contract may also contain requirements for naming your puppy, details of the puppy's health, and a stipulation regarding what will happen if you can no longer take care of the animal. (The dog is usually returned to the breeder.) Information concerning the steps that will be taken if the new owner is negligent or abusive to the dog is also included in the contract.

Health Tests And Certifications

A healthy puppy requires healthy parents and a clean genetic history, which is a bit more difficult to guarantee in a Schnoodle due to the brief history of this breed. A breed with so many potential genetic issues, like the Schnoodle, needs a breeder who seriously follows good breeding practices. A conscientious breeder keeps extensive records for each puppy and for their parents. You should review each of the parents' complete histories to understand what traits your puppy is likely to inherit. Pay attention to temperament, learning traits, attachment issues, and any other personality trait you consider important. You can either request these documents be sent to you electronically, or you can pick them up when you visit the breeder in person.

It might be time-consuming to review the breeder's information for each parent, but it is always well worth the time. The more you know about the parents, the better prepared you will be for your puppy.

All breeders should ensure their Schnauzers undergo the following health tests:

- Cardiac Exam (Miniature Schnauzer)
- DCM DNA Test (Standard Schnauzer)
- Hip Evaluation (Giant and Standard Schnauzer)
- Ophthalmologist Evaluation (all three Schnauzer sizes)
- Thyroid Evaluation (Giant Schnauzer)

All breeders should ensure their Poodles undergo the following health tests:

- Hip Evaluation (Standard and Miniature Poodles)
- Ophthalmologist Evaluation (all three Poodle sizes)
- Patella Evaluation (Miniature and Toy Poodles)
- PRA Optigen DNA Test (Miniature and Toy Poodles)

Photo Courtesy
of Maureen Lemmon

Selecting A Puppy From A Breeder

"From a breeder, my highest recommendation would be to make sure you are buying from someone who raises the dogs and the puppies in their home. Your puppies will get a lot more attention by doing so and will be well socialized. If you rescue from a shelter, make sure they have temperament testing done before you bring them home to make sure they are a good fit for you and your family."

ANGELA DENNY
Angela's Schnoodles

Selecting your puppy should be done in person. However, if the breeder is willing to share videos and pictures, you can start checking out your puppy immediately after he is born!

You should consider the following steps once you are allowed to visit the puppy in person:

- Assess the group of puppies as a whole. If most or all of the puppies are aggressive or fearful, this is an indication of a problem with the litter or (more likely) the breeder. The following are considered red flags if they are displayed by a majority of the puppies:
  - Tucked tails
  - Shrinking away from people
  - Whimpering when people get close
  - Constant attacking of your hands or feet (beyond pouncing)
- Notice how each puppy plays with the other puppies in the litter. This is a great indicator of how your puppy will react to any pets you already have at home.
- Notice which puppies greet you first and which puppies hang back to observe you from afar.
- Puppies should not be over or underweight. A swollen stomach is generally a sign of worms or other health problems.
- Puppies should have straight, sturdy legs. Splayed legs can be a sign that there is something wrong.
- Examine the puppy's ears for mites, which will cause a discharge if present. The inside of the ear should be pink, not red or inflamed.
- The eyes should be clear and bright.

- Check the puppy's mouth for pink, healthy-looking gums.
- Pet the puppy to check his coat for the following:
  - Be sure the coat feels thick and full. If the breeder has allowed the fur to get matted or dirty, it is an indication they are likely not taking proper care of the animals.
  - Check for fleas and mites by running your hand from the head to the tail; then, under the tail - fleas are more likely to hide under a dog's tail. If mites are present, they may look like dandruff.
- Check the puppy's rump for redness and sores; try to check the puppy's last bowel movement to ensure its firmness.

Pick the puppy that exhibits the personality traits you want in your dog. If you want a forward, friendly, excitable dog, the first puppy to greet you may be the one you choose. If you want a dog that will think things through and let others get more attention, look for a puppy that sits back and observes before approaching you.

CHAPTER 4
Planning For Your New Schnoodle

Preparing for your Schnoodle to come home is exciting! You will have a sizable number of tasks that must be completed before your new dog arrives. This chapter will discuss the initial steps to take before bringing home your new family addition!

Photo Courtesy
of Jordan Drake

Planning The First Year's Budget

Caring for a puppy is a lot more expensive than you might think! You will definitely want a budget, which is a good reason to start purchasing supplies a few months in advance. When you buy the items you need, you will begin to formulate an idea of how much money you will spend each month. Of course, there are some items that are one-time purchases, but many other items, like food and treats, will have to be purchased regularly.

The following table will help you plan your budget. Keep in mind the prices are rough estimates and may be significantly different based on your location.

Item	Considerations	Estimated Costs
Crate	You may need two crates: one for the puppy and one for when the puppy grows up, unless the dog will remain small. This should be a comfortable space where the puppy will sleep and rest, so you should not get a large crate for a puppy.	Wire crate: $60 to $350 Portable crate: $35 to $200
Bed	You may need two beds: one for the puppy and one for when the pup grows up. This will be placed in the crate.	$10 to $55
Leash	It should be short in the beginning because you need to be able to keep your puppy from getting overexcited and running to the end of a long line.	Short leash: $6 to $15 Retractable: $8 to $25
Doggie bags for walks	If you walk at dog parks, this won't be necessary. For those who don't have daily access to bags, it is best to purchase packs to ensure you don't run out.	Singles cost less than $1 each. Packs: $4 to $16
Collar	You may need two collars: one for a puppy and one for an adult Schnoodle.	$10 to $30

Tags	These will likely be provided by your vet. Find out what information the vet provides for tags; then, purchase any tags that are not provided. At a minimum, your Schnoodle should have tags with your address on it in case the pup escapes.	Contact your vet before purchasing to see if the required rabies tags include your contact info.
Puppy food	The larger the bag, the higher the cost but the fewer times you will need to purchase food. You will need to purchase specific puppy food in the beginning. Adult dog food is more expensive, particularly for large breeds, like some of the larger Schnoodles.	$9 to $90 per bag
Water and food bowls	These will need to be kept in the puppy's area. If you have other dogs, you will need separate bowls for the puppy.	$10 to $40
Toothbrush/ Toothpaste	You will need to brush teeth regularly so plan to use more than one toothbrush during the first year.	$2.50 to $14
Hairbrush	Schnoodle coats are incredibly easy to maintain, but you should still brush them regularly. When they are puppies, brushing offers a fantastic way to bond.	$3.50 to $20
Toys	You definitely want to get toys for your puppy; you will also want toys for more aggressive chewers, especially if your puppy goes through them quickly. You will want to buy your adult Schnoodle toys for play (cost of adult dog toys not included).	$2.00 Packs of toys range from $10 to $20 (which is easier in the long run as your pup will chew through toys quickly)
Training treats	You will need treats from the beginning and likely won't need to change the treats based on your Schnoodle's age; you may need to change treats to keep your dog's interest, however.	$4.50 to $15

You won't need to immediately purchase the adult version of these items, but you will need to buy them within the first six months because your puppy will grow quickly! Establish a budget for the initial costs; then, create a second budget for adult-versions of these items as your puppy grows.

Preparing Your Children

In order to make your puppy feel comfortable in his new home, you must make sure your children are careful and gentle with the dog whether you adopt a puppy or an adult dog. A Schnoodle is a breed that looks absolutely adorable, and some kids may try to treat the puppy like a toy or a stuffed animal, which could be detrimental to your dog. You should make sure your children follow all of the "puppy rules" from the very beginning to ensure your puppy feels safe, happy, and isn't accidentally injured. Schnoodles already tend to be wary of kids, so you need to make sure your dog has no reason to be uncomfortable around your children.

The following are the Five Golden Rules your children should follow from day one:

1. Always be gentle and respectful.
2. Do not disturb the puppy during mealtime.
3. Chase is an outside game.
4. The Schnoodle should always remain firmly on the ground.
5. Never pick him up.
6. All valuables should be kept out of the puppy's reach.

Since your kids are going to ask why these rules are necessary, the following are some explanations you can use. If necessary, you can simplify them for younger children or for a dialogue with teens.

Always Be Gentle And Respectful

Little Schnoodle puppies are ridiculously cute and cuddly, but they are also more fragile than adults. At no time should anyone play roughly with a puppy or an adult Schnoodle! It is important to be respectful of your puppy to help him learn to also be respectful toward people and other animals.

This rule must be applied consistently every time your children play with your puppy. Be firm if you see your children getting too excited or rough. You don't want the puppy to get overly excited either because he might end up nipping or biting someone. If he does, it won't be his fault because he is still learning as a puppy. Make sure your children understand the possible repercussions if they get too rough.

Photo Courtesy of Tanya Banse

Mealtime

Schnoodles, like nearly every breed, can be protective of their food, especially if you rescue a dog that has previously had to fend for himself. Even if you have a puppy, you don't want him to feel insecure during his mealtime because he will learn to be aggressive whenever he eats. Save yourself, your family, and your dog from problems by making sure mealtime is your dog's time alone. Teach your children their own mealtime is off limits to the puppy, as well. No feeding him from the table!

Chase

Make sure your children understand why a game of Chase is perfect for the outdoors (though you'll need to monitor things), but inside the house, Chase is off limits!

Running inside your home gives your Schnoodle puppy the impression your home isn't safe for him because he is being chased; it also teaches your puppy that running indoors is allowed, which can be dangerous as the dog gets older and bigger. One of the last things you want to see is your adult Schnoodle go barreling through your home - knocking into people and furniture - because it was fine for him to run in the house when he was a puppy!

Paws On The Ground

Even though you might want to carry your new family member around or play with the pup like a baby, you and your family will have to resist that urge. Kids particularly have trouble understanding this idea because they might see the puppy as being more like a toy than a living creature. The younger your children are, the more difficult it will be for them to understand the difference. It is so tempting to treat the puppy like a baby by carrying him around in your arms, but this is incredibly uncomfortable and unhealthy for the puppy.

Older children will quickly learn that a puppy's nip or bite hurts a lot more than one would think. Those little teeth are quite sharp, and if he nips at you, he could accidently be dropped – no one wants that to happen. If your children are never allowed to pick up the puppy, things will be a lot better for everyone involved. Remember, this also applies to you, so don't make things difficult by doing something you constantly tell your children not to do.

Keep Valuables Out Of Reach

Valuables are not something that should end up in your puppy's mouth - whether they are toys, jewelry, or shoes. Your kids will be less than happy if their personal possessions are chewed up by an inquisitive puppy, so teach them to put toys, clothes, and other valuables far out of the puppy's reach.

Preparing Your Current Pets

Schnoodles are equal-opportunity adorers – they love to love the people and dogs who live with them! You should start socializing them with your other dogs or pets when they are puppies. In most cases, this is a fairly straightforward process as long as your pets are comfortable with you bringing a puppy into their home.

The following are important tasks you should complete when preparing your current pets for the new arrival:

- Set a schedule for activities and the people who will need to participate.
- Preserve your current dog's favorite places and furniture; make sure their toys and their items are not in the puppy's space.
- Have playdates at your home to observe your dog(s) reactions to having an addition to the house.

Stick To A Schedule

Obviously, the puppy is going to receive a lot of attention in the beginning, so you need to make a concerted effort to be sure your current pets know you will still and care for them. Set a specific time in your schedule when you can show your current dog(s) how much you love them and make sure you don't stray from that schedule after the puppy arrives.

When you bring the puppy home, plan to have at least one adult present for each dog you have in your home. Cats are a cause for concern, so you will need an extra adult – to watch the cat – when your puppy arrives, especially if you adopt an adult Schnoodle.

Having a schedule in place for your other dogs will make it easier to follow the plan with the puppy. Schnoodles love to be prepared for what is about to happen - at least in the beginning.

Once he has arrived, your puppy is going to eat, sleep, and spend most of the day and night in his assigned space. This means your puppy's space cannot block your current canine's favorite furniture, bed, or anywhere he rests during the day. None of your

SCHNOODLES IN BOOKS

Oliver the Schnoodle

Oliver the Schnoodle is a conceptual book for kids and grown-ups alike. Photographed by Marta Elena Vassilakis, a fashion and beauty photographer based in New York and Los Angeles, the book depicts her beloved Schnoodle, Oliver, in a variety of real-life situations. More information can be found at olivertheschnoodle.com.

Photo Courtesy
of Lynette Eckroat

current dog's "stuff" should be in the puppy's area either; this includes toys. You don't want your dog to feel as if the puppy is taking over his territory. Make sure your children also understand to never to put your current dog's things in the puppy's area!

Your dog and your puppy will need to be kept apart in the beginning (even if they seem friendly) until your puppy has received his vaccinations. Puppies are more susceptible to illness during these early days, so wait until the puppy is protected from possible diseases before the dogs spend time together. Leaving the puppy in his puppy space will keep them separated during this critical time.

Helping Your Dog Prepare – Extra At Home Playdates

The following explains strategies that will help prepare your current pooch for the arrival of your puppy:

- Think about your current dog's personality, which will help you decide how to prepare for your new puppy. Each dog is unique, so consider the personality of your dog and predict what might happen when the puppy arrives. If your current dog loves other dogs, this will probably hold true when the puppy shows up. If your current dog is territorial, you will need to be cautious when introducing the two dogs, at least until the Schnoodle has become part of the pack. Excitable dogs need special attention to keep from getting agitated when a new dog comes home. You don't want them to be so excited they make the Schnoodle feel threatened.

- Consider the times when unfamiliar dogs have been in your home. How did your current dog react to these other furry visitors? If your canine became territorial, be cautious when introducing your new pup. If you have never invited another dog into your home, organize a playdate with other dogs before your Schnoodle puppy arrives. You need to know how your current furry babies will react to new dogs in the house so you can properly prepare. Meeting a dog at home is quite different from encountering one outside the home.

- Think about your dog's interactions with other dogs for as long as you have known him. Has your dog shown protective or possessive behavior, either with you or others? Food is one of the reasons dogs will display aggression because they don't want anyone eating what is theirs. Some dogs can be protective of people and toys, too.

- If you know someone who owns a Schnoodle, organize a playdate so your current dog becomes aware of the temperament of a Schnoodle. If not, a playdate with a guard-dog, such as a German Shephard, Akita, Cane Corso, Doberman Pinscher, or Rottweiler, could be arranged. Every dog is different, but guardian breeds have similar temperaments, includ-ing a wariness of others, so this may help your dog learn how to be more measured in his approach to a Schnoodle. Of course, if you are bringing a puppy home, this will not be as much of a concern, but it could still be helpful.

These same rules apply, no matter how many dogs you have. Think about their individual personalities, as well as how they interact together. Similar to humans, you may find when your dogs are together, they act dif-ferently. This is something you will need to keep in mind as you plan their first introduction. (Details of how to introduce your current dog(s) and your new puppy - plus how to juggle the two new personalities – are included in Chapter 8.)

CHAPTER 5
Preparing Your Home And Your Schedule

Whether you acquire an adult dog or a puppy, you will have your work cut out for you when preparing your home. Most importantly, your home needs to be secure, both to protect your new canine and yourself. Clever breeds, like the Schnoodle, are likely to explore from the moment they walk through the door. They will immediately start to figure out how to get into things and around barriers!

Plan to conduct several "house checks" in the week leading up to your puppy or your dog's arrival. Be sure your new Schnoodle has a safe space, which includes all of the essentials and makes your newest family member's arrival a fun time for everyone!

Photo Courtesy
of Lara Sanders

Whether bringing home a puppy or an adult Schnoodle, it is like preparing for the arrival of an incredibly headstrong toddler. The new addition will need convincing there is a good reason to listen to you! Schnoodles should learn that you are in control, but you have to gain their respect before they will follow your command. Even after that, they may not want to listen to you all of the time. If your current dog already grabs food, climbs on furniture, and disregards your restrictions, training your new puppy will be difficult. Dog-proofing your home will help you keep your dog safe while he is learning to listen to your words.

Creating A Safe Space For Your Dog Or Puppy

Your puppy will need a dedicated space that includes a crate, food and water bowls, pee pads, and toys. All of these things will need to be in the area where the puppy will stay when you are not able to give him attention. The puppy's space should be gated so your Schnoodle cannot get out and young children (or dogs) cannot get in. It should be a safe space where the puppy can see you going about your usual business and feel comfortable.

Crates

Crate training can be fairly easy, but not if you have a crate that is too big, too small, or too uncomfortable for your dog to feel like it is a safe place. To make training easier, be sure the puppy's crate and bedding are set up and ready before your puppy arrives.

Never treat the crate like it is a prison for your puppy. It's meant to be a safe haven after overstimulation or when it's time to sleep. Ensure your dog never associates the crate with punishment or negative emotions. The crate should be adjustable so you can make it a bit larger when your puppy becomes an adult. You can also get your puppy a carrying crate in the early days to make trips to the vet a little easier. A smaller crate will not work when your Schnoodle is an adult, but a carrying crate has plenty of space for a puppy.

As mentioned in an earlier chapter, a crate can be used to help with housetraining. The Schnoodle is one of the easier breeds to housetrain, which is a welcome piece of news! You may want to have a pee pad in an area several feet away from the puppy's crate so he can go to the bathroom while keeping the area around his bed clean. Make sure to find out from the breeder if the puppy has already begun housetraining. If he is already making progress, you may not want to add the pee pad since that can be confusing to the puppy.

Puppy-Proof The House

The most dangerous rooms and items in your home will be as dangerous to your puppy as if he was a little baby. The biggest difference is your Schnoodle is going to become mobile much faster than a child. He will get into dangerous situations immediately if you don't eliminate all the hazards before his arrival. Be aware that puppies will try to eat virtually anything! Nothing is safe – not even your furniture – and they will also gnaw on wood and metal. Anything within their reach is considered fair game! Keep this in mind as you go about puppy-proofing your home.

Plant Dangers

You will also need to be mindful of the plants in and around your home that could be hazardous to your dog. The following are thirty-four kinds of plants that should not be within your dog's reach. Remember to check both inside and outside your home:

Mildly Toxic	Mildly to Moderately Toxic	Moderately Toxic	Moderately to Highly Toxic	Highly Toxic
Asparagus Fern	Aloe	Alocasia	Cactus	Brunfelsia
Begonia	Amaryllis	Arrowhead	Kalanchoe	Desert Rose
Ficus Benjamina	Calla Lilly	Dieffenbachia		Flame Lily
Flamingo Flower	Cyclamen	Dracaena Fragrans		Kafir Lily
Gardenia	Dracaena	English Ivy		Oleander
Geranium	Philodendron	Eucalyptus		Sago Palm
Golden Pothos		Peyote		Bird of Paradise (Strelitzia)
Jade Plant				
Schefflera				
Ti Plant				
ZZ Plant				

Indoor Hazards And Fixes

This section explains where you should focus your "dog-proofing" attention inside your home. In case of problems, be sure your vet's number is posted on the fridge and in at least one other room in the house. If you do this before your pup arrives, it will be there if you need it. Even if the number is programmed into your phone, family members or dog-sitters will need to see the vet's number conveniently posted.

A Schnoodle will be an avid explorer, wanting to get into everything if given the opportunity. Get on your hands and knees and see each room from your Schnoodle's perspective - you will find at least one thing you missed previously.

Hazards	Fixes	Time Estimate
Kitchen		
Poisons	Keep in secure, childproof cabinets or on high shelves.	30 min.
Trash Cans	Use a lockable trash can or keep it in a secure location.	10 min.
Appliances	Make sure all cords are out of reach.	15 min.
Human Food	Keep out of reach.	Constant (Start making it a habit!)
Floors		
Slippery Surfaces	Put down rugs or special mats designed to stick to the floor.	30 min. – 1 hour
Training Area	Train on non-slip surfaces.	Constant
Bathrooms		
Toilet Brush	Either have one that locks into the container or keep it out of reach.	5 min./ bathroom
Poisons	Keep in secure, childproof cabinets or on high shelves.	15 – 30 min./ bathroom
Toilets	Keep lids closed. Do not use automatic toilet-cleaning chemicals.	Constant (Start making it a habit!)
Cabinets	Keep locked with childproof locks.	15 – 30 min./ bathroom

Laundry Room		
Clothing	Store clean and dirty clothing off the floor and out of reach.	15 – 30 min.
Poisons (bleach, pods/detergent, dryer sheets, and misc. poisons)	Keep in secure, childproof cabinets or on high shelves.	15 min.
Around the Home		
Plants	Keep off the floor.	45 min. – 1 hour
Trash Cans	Have a lockable trash can or keep it in a secure location.	30 min.
Electrical Cords/ Window Blind Cords	Hide them or make sure they are out of reach; pay particular attention to entertainment and computer areas.	1.5 hours
Poisons	Check to make sure there aren't any in reach (WD40, window/screen cleaner, carpet cleaner, air fresheners); move all poisons to a central, locked location.	1 hour
Windows	Be sure cords are out of reach in all rooms.	1 – 2 hours
Fireplaces	Store cleaning supplies and tools where the puppy can't get into them; Cover the fireplace opening with something the puppy can't knock over.	10 min./ fireplace
Stairs	Cordon off so that your puppy can't go up or down the stairs; make sure to test all puppy gates for safety.	10 – 15 min.
Coffee Tables/ End Tables/ Nightstands	Clear of dangerous objects (e.g. scissors, sewing equipment, pens, and pencils) and all valuables.	30 – 45 min.

If you have a cat, keep the litter box off the floor. It needs to be somewhere that your cat can easily get to it but your Schnoodle cannot. Since this involves training your cat, it's something you should do well in advance of the puppy's arrival. You don't want your cat to undergo too many significant changes all at once...the puppy will be enough of a disruption! If your cat associates the change with the puppy, you may find the feline refusing to use the litter box.

Outdoor Hazards And Fixes

This section explains the areas that need your attention outside your home. Remember to post the vet's number in one of the sheltered areas in case of an emergency.

Hazards	Fixes	Time Estimate
Garage		
Poisons	Keep in secure, childproof cabinets or on high shelves (e.g., car chemicals, cleaning supplies, paint, lawn care) – this includes fertilizer.	1 hour
Trash Bins	Keep them in a secure location.	5 min.
Tools (e.g. lawn, car, hardware, power tools)	Make sure all cords are kept out of reach and never hang over the side of surfaces.	30 min. – 1 hour
Equipment (e.g. sports, fishing)	Keep out of reach and never hang over the side of surfaces.	Constant (Start making it a habit!)
Sharp Implements	Keep out of reach and never hang over the side of surfaces.	30 min.
Bikes	Store off the ground or in a place the Schnoodle cannot get to (to keep the pup from biting the tires).	20 min.
Fencing (Can Be Done Concurrently)		
Breaks	Fix any breaks in the fencing. You need to make sure your Schnoodle can't easily get out of your yard.	30 min. – 1 hour
Gaps	Fill any gaps, even if they are intentional, so your Schnoodle doesn't escape.	30 min. – 1 hour

Holes/Dips at Base	Fill any area that can be easily crawled under.	1 – 2 hours
Yard		
Poisons	Don't leave any poisons in the yard.	1 – 2 hours
Plants	Verify that low plants aren't poisonous; fence off anything that is (such as grape vines).	45 min. – 1 hour
Tools (e.g. lawn, maintenance, and gardening tools)	Make sure they are out of reach; make sure nothing is hanging over the sides of outdoor tables.	30 min. – 1 hour

Never leave your Schnoodle alone in the garage even when he is an adult. Your puppy will be in the garage when you take car trips, which is why it is important to puppy-proof this area, also.

Some Schnoodles are diggers so make sure there are not any good starting points where your dog can crawl under the fence. Leaving your dog in the yard without supervision is a good way to end up with holes where your flowers used to be. Odds are your dog will try to bury something he loves for a later time. Since a Schnoodle sees nothing wrong with digging in the dirt, there's no reason to get mad at him. Angry emotions do not work on a Schnoodle! If your dog enjoys digging in the dirt, create a specific space where he can dig; then, encourage this behavior in that particular area. For these reasons, you will need to inspect your fences, at least once every month, after you bring your Schnoodle home.

As with the inside, you will need to check your outdoor preparations by getting down low and inspecting all areas from a puppy's perspective. Again, you are all but guaranteed to find at least one thing you missed.

HELPFUL TIP
Which Brush To Buy?

Schnoodles have a fine fur coat and require regular brushing. The best brush for this type of coat is a slicker brush, which is a type of brush that has stiff metal pins. Regular brushing will not only prevent tangles but can be a good way to bond with your dog.

Photo Courtesy
of Anne Marie Leamey

Choosing Your Veterinarian

You should choose a vet before you bring your dog home because as with any doctor appointment, scheduling a veterinary appointment may take a while. Vets that specialize in a particular breed are scarce, so it might be difficult to arrange the first appointment. You need to find a vet and to book the first appointment well in advance of your dog's arrival.

Whether you bring home a puppy or an adult dog, your canine should see the vet within the first forty-eight hours of his arrival. In fact, twenty-four

Photo Courtesy of Cynthia Gaddis

hours is strongly recommended to make sure your dog is healthy. If there is a vet near you who specializes in or has worked with Schnoodles before, that will be best for your pup.

The following are some things to consider when looking for a vet:

- What is the vet's level of familiarity with Schnoodles?
- The vet doesn't have to be a specialist, but a vet with experience with both of the par ent breeds is your best bet. This type of vet is beneficial since they can help explain what to expect in the different stages of your dog's life. Schnoodles are a popular designer breed, but they are not nearly as common as the parent breeds. In fact, you may not be able to find a vet with much Schnoodle-specific experience. Odds are, however, your vet will have worked with Poodles and Schnauzers before. It won't be a problem if they haven't worked specifically with the designer breed, but it would be helpful.
- How far from your home is the vet?
- You don't want the vet to be more than thirty minutes away in case of an emergency.
- Is the vet available for emergencies after hours, or can they recommend a vet in case of an emergency?
- Is the vet part of a local veterinary hospital, or does the doctor refer patients to a local pet hospital?
- Is the vet one of several partners, or does he work alone? If he or she belongs to a partnership, can your dog see the same vet for all office visits?
- How are appointments booked?
- Can other services be performed at the clinic, such as grooming and boarding?
- Is the vet accredited?
- What is the price for the initial visit? What are the prevailing costs for routine visits that might include such things as shots?
- What tests and checks are performed during the initial visit?
- Can you visit the vet you are considering before you bring your dog home?

If so, inspect the office environment and ask if you can speak to the vet. He or she should be willing to put you at ease and to answer your questions. Even though a vet's time is valuable, they should take a few minutes to help you feel confident about your decision.

CHAPTER 6
Bringing Your Schnoodle Home

"The Schnoodle is one the smartest breeds I have been blessed to work with. That said, they can quickly learn to manipulate their owners. We often want our new puppy to be in our bedroom, but if the new puppy can see you I guarantee they will whine to be let out so they can be with you. The first few nights it is best to put them in a room away from where you are. If you want to feel more connected, buy a cheap baby monitor so you can hear you new puppy if it wakes up!"

CATHERINE WILSON
Oodles of Schnoodles

Photo Courtesy
of Derek & Laura Lieberman

B ringing home a lively, happy dog will be a memory that stays in your mind for years! So, you should enjoy the experience to its fullest by making sure you are well-prepared for the event. (Make sure to read Chapter 7 regarding how to introduce your adult dog to a multi-pet home.)

Schnoodles are known for being friendly to people and dogs, but you should make sure all humans feel comfortable, too. Whether you bring home a puppy or an adult dog, you will need a well- prepared space where no other dogs are allowed. Preferably, where no cats are allowed either. You want to make sure to take it slow in the early days when introducing and socializing your new dog.

Final Preparations And Planning

Most intelligent breeds need a human presence for the first week (and much of the first month) so any escape attempt can be thwarted imme- diately! You should take time from work during the first twenty-four to forty-eight hours; the best-case scenario would have you at home for the first week or two. The more time you dedicate to helping your new little friend become accustomed to his surroundings, the better. These first few days will help your new puppy adjust quickly and will allow your pup to feel comfortable.

Ensure You Have Food And Other Supplies On Hand
The day before your Schnoodle arrives, review the list you created after Chapter 4 and make a quick check to ensure you have everything you need. Take a few moments to consider if there is anything you are missing. This will save you from rushing out for additional supplies after the arrival of your new family member.

Design A Tentative Puppy Schedule
Prepare a tentative schedule to help you get started over the course of the first week. Your days are about to get remarkably busy, so you need somewhere to begin before your puppy arrives.

The following are three key areas to establish before your puppy arrives:
- Feeding
- Training (including housetraining)
- Playing

When you bring home a puppy, you may be expecting a puppy with high energy. However, puppies of any breed (no matter how active they will be

Photo Courtesy
of Lynn Gotsis

later) sleep between eighteen and twenty hours per day. Having a predictable sleep schedule will help your puppy grow up healthier.

In the beginning, you won't need to worry about making sure that your puppy is tired out by the end of the day. His stamina will build fairly quickly, though; by the end of the first year, your pup will be a lot more active! As your pup starts to sleep less and play more, he will need thirty to sixty minutes of daily, physical activity.

In the early days, your puppy's schedule will revolve around sleeping and eating - with some walking and socialization. Waking hours will include training and play.

Do A Quick Final Puppy-Proofing Inspection Before The Puppy Arrives

No matter how busy you are or how carefully you followed the puppy-proofing checklist, you still need to inspect your home one last time. The day before your puppy arrives, be sure to set aside an hour or two to make sure everything is in place.

Initial Meeting

Before the puppy comes home and becomes a distraction, meet with all family members to ensure Chapter 4 rules are understood. This includes knowing how to handle the puppy. Determine who is going to be responsible for primary puppy care and for primary training. To teach younger children responsibility, a parent can pair with a child to manage the puppy's care. The child can be responsible for feeding the puppy and keeping the water bowl filled. Of course, a parent should oversee these tasks.

Picking Up Your Puppy Or Dog And The Ride Home

A good bit of planning and preparation goes into picking up your puppy, especially if you are going to the breeder's home. If possible, do this on a weekend or during a holiday season. This will allow you unrushed, quality time at home with your new puppy. The following section covers the preparation plan and the actual trip home. Chapter 7 will explain what to do if you have other dogs you need to introduce to the puppy.

As tempting as it is to cuddle the puppy in your lap, it is both safer and more comfortable for the puppy if you use a crate for the ride home; two adults should also be present for the ride:

- The crate should be anchored in the car for safety and should include a cushion. If you have a long trip, bring food and water for the puppy and plan to stop at different intervals of the trip. Do not put food and water in the crate as they will not be anchored down; sloshing water can scare your puppy. You can cover the bottom of the crate with a towel or pee pad in case of accidents.

- Call the breeder to make sure everything is still on schedule and make sure the puppy is ready to leave.
- Arrange for the mother dog to leave her scent on a blanket to help make the puppy's transition more comfortable.
- Make sure the second adult will be on time so the two of you can head to the pick-up destination.
- If you have other dogs, make sure all of the adults involved in the introduction process know what to do. They should know the time and place for that first neutral territory meeting.

Photo Courtesy of Koreen Hirakami

If you do not have other dogs, you can pick up your puppy and head straight home. If you have a trip which lasts more than a couple of hours, stop periodically so your puppy can stretch, exercise, drink, and use the bathroom. Do not leave the puppy alone in the car for any amount of time! If you have to use the restroom yourself, at least one adult must remain with the puppy during each stop.

If the puppy has never ridden in a car before, a second person should show the puppy attention while the other person drives. The puppy will be in the crate, but someone can still provide comfort. The puppy will definitely be scared without his mom, siblings, or familiar people to console him. Having an adult present to talk to the puppy will make it less of an ordeal for the little guy.

> ## SCHNOODLES IN BOOKS
> ### *Trudel the Schnoodle*
>
> Written by Jane C. Buseck, *Trudel the Schnoodle: A Children's Book About Obsessive Compulsive Disorder* follows the daily life of Trudel, a dog with obsessive-compulsive dog disorder. Trudel is based on Buseck's family dog, Ru. Jane Buseck holds an M.Ed. in counseling and is a mother of four children, one of whom was diagnosed with OCD by age seven.

This is the time to start teaching your puppy that car trips are enjoyable. This means making sure that the crate is securely anchored; you don't want the crate to slide around while he is helplessly sitting inside. This would be a terrifying experience for the puppy!

When you arrive home, immediately take the puppy or dog outside to use the bathroom. Even if they had an accident in their crate, this is the time to start training your new family member to use the bathroom.

The First Vet Visit And What To Expect

A veterinary visit is necessary within the first two days of your puppy's arrival; in fact, it may be required in the contract with the breeder. The first visit will establish a baseline for the puppy's health. This will also allow the vet to track your puppy's progress and monitor his health as he grows. In addition to providing a chance to ask questions and get advice, this initial assessment will give you more information about your puppy. It also creates an important rapport between your Schnoodle and the vet.

During that first veterinary visit, your pup won't know what to expect. Try to ease his anxiety; you want this first appointment to set a positive tone for all future visits.

The following is a list of several things that must be completed before the day of the appointment:

- Find out how early you need to arrive to complete the paperwork for the new patient.
- Find out if you should bring a stool sample for that first visit. If so, collect it the morning of the visit and make sure to take it with you.
- Bring the paperwork provided by the breeder or rescue organization for the vet to add to your dog's records.

Upon your arrival, your puppy may want to meet the other pups and people in the office. This is something that can be encouraged as long as you keep in mind some basic rules. Although you will need to be mindful, this is an opportunity to socialize the puppy and to create a positive experience with the vet. Before letting your puppy meet other animals, always ask the owner for permission and wait for approval. Most pets at the vet's office are likely to not be feeling well, which means they may not be very affable. You don't want a grumpy, older dog or a sick animal to nip or scare your puppy. Negative social experiences are situations your puppy will remember; they could make a visit to the vet something to dread. Nor do you want your puppy to be exposed to potential illnesses before he has had all his shots.

During the first visit, the vet will conduct an initial assessment of your Schnoodle. One of the most important things the vet will do is weigh your puppy. This is something you are going to have to monitor for your dog's entire life because the breed is prone to obesity. Keep a record of his weight so you can see how quickly your puppy is growing. Ask your vet what is considered a healthy weight for every growth stage and record that as well. Schnoodles grow quickly during their first year; you should still make sure your dog is not gaining more weight than is healthy.

The vet will set the date for the next group of shots, which will likely happen not too long after the initial visit. After receiving vaccinations, prepare for a couple of days of your puppy feeling under the weather.

Crate And Other Preliminary Training

Puppies younger than six months should not be left in a crate for hours at a time. They will not be able to hold their bladders that long, so you must make sure they have a way to get out and to go to the bathroom. If you adopt an adult Schnoodle that is not housetrained, you will need to follow the same rules.

Make sure the crate door is set so it doesn't close on your dog during his initial sniff of the crate. You do not want your Schnoodle to be scared by the door as it is closing behind him; this would make him fearful of the crate in the future.

The following are some suggestions:

- Use a positive, cheerful voice as you let your Schnoodle sniff the crate for the first time. The first experience in the crate should be associated with excitement and positive emotions. Be sure your dog understands the crate is a good place. If you have a blanket from the puppy's mother, put it in the crate to help provide an extra sense of comfort.

- Drop a couple of treats into the crate if your canine seems reluctant to enter. Do NOT force your dog into the crate! If your dog refuses to go all the way into the crate, that is perfectly fine. It has to be HIS decision to enter so it doesn't become a negative experience.

- For a week or two, feed your dog while he is in the crate. Besides keeping the food away from any other pets, this will create positive emotions when entering the crate.

  - If your dog appears comfortable with the crate, put the food all the way at the back of the crate.

  - If not, place the food bowl in the front; then, move it further back in the crate over time.

- Start closing the door once your dog appears to be eating comfortably in the crate. When the food is gone, open the crate door immediately.

- Leave the door closed for longer periods of time after your dog has finished eating. If your pup begins to whine, you know you have left your Schnoodle in the crate for too long.

- Crate your dog for longer periods of time once he shows no signs of discomfort in the crate when he is eating. Train him to go into the crate by simply saying, "Crate" or "Bed." Then, praise your dog and let him know that he has done an excellent job!

Repeat this for several weeks until your dog feels comfortable in his crate. By doing this several times each day, your dog will learn the crate is not a punishment and everything is all right. Initially, you should do this while you are still at home or when you go out to get the mail. When you leave the room and your puppy lasts half an hour without whining, you can leave your pup alone for longer periods of time. However, keep this "absent time" to no more than an hour in the beginning.

During the first few weeks, you should begin to housetrain and extinguish undesirable behavior. Basic training is vital from the start. However, you should let some time pass before taking your new puppy to structured training classes. Instead, wait until he has all of his vaccinations. Knowledgeable trainers will not accept puppies in their classes until your dog's first full round of shots is complete. (Chapters 10 and 12 provide a closer look at how to begin and how to follow through on your puppies training at home.)

Photo Courtesy
of Maureen Lemmon

First Night Frights

That first night is going to be scary for your little Schnoodle puppy! As understandable as this may be, there is only so much comfort you can give your new family member. The more you respond to cries and whimpering, the more he will learn negative behavior provides the desired results. You need to prepare for a balancing act – one that reassures he is safe while keeping him from associating crying with receiving attention from you.

Create a sleeping area for your puppy near where you sleep. The area should have the puppy's bed tucked safely into his crate. This will offer him a safe place to hide and a place where he will feel more comfortable in this strange new home. The entire area should be blocked off to be sure no one can get in (and the puppy can't get out) during the night. This sleeping area should also be close to where people sleep so the puppy doesn't feel abandoned. If you were able to get a blanket or pillow that smells like the mother, make sure this is in your puppy's space. Consider adding a little white noise to cover unfamiliar sounds that could scare your new pet.

Your puppy will make noises over the course of the night. Don't move the puppy away even if the whimpering keeps you awake. If you give in, over time the whimpering, whining, and crying will only become louder. Being moved away from people will only scare the puppy more, reinforcing the anxiety he feels. When your puppy whines during the night, he is not whimpering because he's been in the crate too long. He's scared or wants someone to be with him – he's probably never been alone at night before coming to live with you. Spare yourself trouble later on by teaching the puppy that whimpering will not get him out of the crate. Over time, being close to you at night will be enough to reassure your puppy that everything will be fine.

In the beginning, puppies will need to go to the bathroom every two to three hours. This means you will also need to get up during the night! Make sure your puppy understands he must always go to the bathroom outside before bedtime or on the pee pad. If you ignore this rule, you will have a tough time training him to only relieve himself outside and not in the house.

If you choose to let your dog on the bed, wait until he is housetrained. Otherwise, you might have to replace your mattress within a short time. It is best to simply keep your Schnoodle off the furniture, so he doesn't get hurt and your furniture doesn't get ruined!

CHAPTER 7
The Multi-Pet Household

S chnoodles are an easy breed to bring into the home because most of them love other people and other dogs. They may be a little hesitant at first, but odds are, they will warm up to your other dogs rather quickly.

There are many benefits to already having a dog living in your home. If you own a socialized adult dog, your current dog can help teach your new Schnoodle the rules, and if your current dog is very patient, he could become a mentor to your puppy.

When your Schnoodle sees your dog listening to your commands, he will imitate this behavior and learn the importance of listening. Remember, this

Photo Courtesy of Julie Johnson

works both ways! If your current dog displays negative behavior, you should try to correct these habits before your puppy arrives. You don't want your Schnoodle pup learning bad habits from your current dog!

It is difficult to predict how your new Schnoodle will react to a cat in your home. Some Schnoodles have a high prey drive, while others have little. To see how your Schnoodle reacts to a running creature, you will need to carefully read the following sections.

Introducing Your New Puppy To Your Other Pets

Always introduce all new dogs to your current dog or dogs, regardless of age, in a neutral place away from your home. Even if you have never had problems with your current dog, you are about to change his world. When introducing your dog to the new puppy, select a park or other public area so your dog will not feel territorial. This gives both animals the opportunity to meet and to become familiar with each other on even ground.

When introducing the two, make sure you have at least one other adult with you so there's one person for each canine. If you have more than two dogs, then you should have one adult per dog. This will make it easier to keep all of the dogs under control. Even the best dogs can get excited about meeting a puppy. One of the people who needs to be at this meeting is the person who is in charge of the pets in your home. This helps establish the pack hierarchy.

Don't hold your puppy when the dogs meet. While you may want to protect the puppy, holding him has the opposite effect. Instead, your puppy will feel trapped, but if the puppy is on the ground, he can run if he feels the need to run. Stand near the puppy with your feet a little bit apart, so he can hide behind your legs if he decides he needs to escape.

All dogs should have a few minutes to sniff each other, making sure there is always some slack in each leash. This will help the dogs feel more relaxed, and they won't feel like you are trying to restrain them. Your dog will either want to play, or he might simply ignore the puppy. If the dogs want to play, be careful your current dog doesn't accidentally hurt the puppy, and if your dog ends up ignoring the puppy after an initial sniff, that is fine, too. If your dog is clearly unhappy, keep all dogs apart until everyone is comfortable with the meeting. Don't force the situation.

This introduction could take a while, depending on each individual dog's personality. The friendlier and more accepting your dog is, the easier it will be to incorporate your new puppy into the home. For some dogs, a week is enough time to start feeling comfortable together. For other dogs, it could take a couple of months before they are fully accepting of a new puppy.

SCHNOODLES IN BOOKS

The Adventures of Otto Von Schnoodle

Written by Grace Birch, *The Adventures of Otto Von Schnoodle* is a photobook trilogy following an adorable Schnoodle based on Birch's dog. Grace Birch is a community advocate living in Florida and hopes to inspire children to read with her dog's charming adventures.

Since this is a completely new dynamic for your dog, he may be angry with you for bringing this bundle of energy into his life. This is enough to make anyone unhappy - especially a dog that has grown accustomed to a certain lifestyle.

The older your current dog, the more likely it is that a puppy will be an unwelcome addition. Older dogs can get cranky around a puppy that doesn't know when enough is enough! The goal is to make your puppy feel welcome and safe and to let your older dog know that your love for him is as strong as ever.

Once your new family member and the rest of the canine pack become acquainted and comfortable, you can head home. When you arrive, take the dogs into the yard and remove the leashes. Again, you will need one adult per dog, including the puppy. If the dogs are all right or are indifferent to the puppy, you can let your dog inside. Then, re-leash the puppy, keeping him on the leash as you go inside. Of course, this happens after showing him where he should do his business!

Put the puppy in the puppy area when the introductions are complete. Remember to make sure your current dog cannot get into this area and your puppy cannot get out.

Introducing An Adult Dog To Other Pets

Always approach the introduction (and first few weeks together) with caution. The new adult Schnoodle will need his own things from the very beginning. When you aren't around, your dog should be kept in a separate area so there won't be any fighting among the dogs. If your dogs play rough and show no interest in establishing a boss, it will be easier for your new Schnoodle to fit into the pack.

Plan for this introduction to take at least an hour. Since the dogs are both adults, they will need to move and to become acquainted at their own pace.

When introducing your current dog(s) to your new dog, follow the same steps as you would with a puppy:

- Begin in neutral territory.
- Ask one adult to be present for each adult canine during the introduction.
- Introduce one dog at a time – don't let several dogs meet your new Schnoodle all at once.

Bring treats to the meeting of two adult dogs – unlike with puppies. The animals will respond to the treats, and if the atmosphere becomes tense, the treats will create a distraction.

During the introduction, watch the Schnoodle and your dogs to see if any of them raises his hackles. This is one of the first obvious signs that a dog is uncomfortable. If the Schnoodle's hackles are up, back off the introductions for a little bit. Do this by calling your current dog back first. This is also when you should start waving treats around! Avoid pulling on the leashes to separate the dogs. You don't want to add physical tension to the situation because that could trigger a fight. Treats will work for all dogs and calling their names should help get things under control.

If any of the dogs are showing their teeth or growling, call your dog back and give the dogs a chance to settle down. Use treats and a calming voice to get them to relax. You want all the dogs to feel comfortable during the first meeting, so don't force the friendship. If they seem uncomfortable or wary at first, let them move at their own pace.

Older Dogs And Your Schnoodle

If your current dog is older, keep in mind puppies are energetic, and they want to engage older dogs in their play. This can be very trying for your older canine, so make sure your older dog doesn't get too tired of the puppy's antics. A tired, older dog could snap and nip at your puppy in hopes of getting a little rest. You don't want your puppy to begin snapping at other dogs, too. Watch for signs your older dog is ready for some alone time, some time with you, or simply a break from the puppy.

You should always make sure your older dog has safe places where he can be alone. This is essential for those times he just doesn't feel up to being around a spry, young puppy! By keeping your puppy and your older dog separate, this should prevent constant scolding plus the puppy will not become wary of older dogs.

Even if you own an adult Schnoodle, he might be too energetic for your older dog to handle. Schnoodles tend to be active dogs whether they are puppies or adults! Be mindful and make sure your dog's golden years are not marred by a new canine that wants to play in a way your older dog can't.

Dog Aggression And Territorial Behavior

If your Schnoodle takes after the Schnauzer side of the family, you could see some aggressive or territorial behavior. This isn't a terrible trait since this makes for a fantastic watchdog. Yet, it does mean you will need to take the time to train and socialize your Schnoodle. When people come to visit, your Schnoodle may want to protect his pack, so you will need to tell your guests how to interact with your new family member.

If your Schnoodle feels that someone poses a threat, he may react aggressively. It is easier to train against aggressive behavior while your dog is young. However, an aggressive older dog should be monitored closely and should not be left alone with other pets or children. An older Schnoodle has to learn how to be a part of the pack and the proper way to react to people while playing with toys and other items. This is why it is essential to always be firm and consistent.

Do not use choke chains or other negative reinforcers on your Schnoodle! Not only do these hurt your dog, but a Schnoodle does not react well to negative reinforcement because he is a very independent thinker. These types of restraints teach your dog you are not in control, and you are using a choke chain to force a certain behavior upon him. What does work is treats and removing the dog from any negative situation. Reward your dog for his good behavior, and every time your dog does what you ask him to do...reward him. (Details in how to train your Schnoodle are discussed in Chapter 12.)

Dealing with Dominance Aggression:

- Dominance aggression is when your dog wants to show control over another animal or person. This kind of aggression can be seen in the following behaviors and in reaction to anyone going near the Schnoodle's belongings (like toys or a food bowl):

  - Growling
  - Nipping
  - Snapping

This is the behavior that the pack leader uses to warn others not to touch his stuff. If you see this reaction in your Schnoodle while around you, a family member, or another pet, you must intervene immediately. Correct him by saying, "No," then lavish him with praise when he stops. Remember, you must consistently intervene whenever your Schnoodle behaves in this manner.

Do not leave your Schnoodle alone with other people, dogs, or animals as long as any dominance aggression is exhibited. If you are not there to intervene, your dog will push boundaries and will likely try to show his dominance over those around him. Never train your Schnoodle to react aggressively!

Once you are sure this behavior has been eliminated, you can leave your dog and Schnoodle alone for short periods of time. You should remain in another room or somewhere in close proximity but out of sight. Over time,

Photo Courtesy
of Renae Facundus

you can leave your pets alone when you get the mail; then, try leaving them when you run errands or longer tasks. Eventually, you will be able to leave your Schnoodle alone with other dogs without worrying that he will show dominance to others.

Well-socialized males are more interested in meeting and greeting other dogs, but unsocialized males can be aggressive and domineering. Females tend to be more predictable. They are aloof when socialized, and when not socialized, they are less likely to be aggressive or domineering.

Your Schnoodle must learn your home does not belong to him alone. It belongs to people and other pets as well, and he is a part of the home... not the boss!

Natural Prey Drive

Schnauzers were originally bred to help on the farm, including chasing and eliminating prey; smaller poodles are also driven to chase prey though usually to a lesser extent. As such, there is no way to know what your Schnoodle's reaction will be to seeing a running animal. If your pooch takes after the Schnauzer, you will need to be very vigilant during walks and when introducing your dog to cats or other small pets.

To keep your current pets safe, you must prepare for the possibility your Schnoodle will chase these small animals. You will need to socialize your Schnoodle puppy with the cat long before the puppy runs free in the home. Always be present when they interact so you can correct the puppy's behavior, particularly if the puppy tries to chase the cat.

If you have other small animals, they will need to be kept in areas where your Schnoodle cannot go. Rabbits, rodents, ferrets, and other pets are not usually trainable. Most small animals aren't able to learn not to run away, which your puppy will likely take as an invitation to play. He might kill the small animal because that is what centuries of Schnauzer breeding have taught him to do. Remember that Schnoodles are clever and, with their height (at least the bigger ones), they can reach a lot of things. Having a door between your dog and your smaller animals will be the safest thing for everyone.

If you have a yard, it should be enclosed by fencing - in case your dog shows his Schnauzer side and decides to chase something. It should be an actual fence, not an electric one, since your Schnoodle could run right through it if he has a strong enough prey drive. If you don't have a fence, your dog may be so focused on chasing small creatures that he might run into the street. No one wants that to happen!

Feeding Time Practices

Your Schnoodle puppy will be fed in his puppy space, so mealtime will not be a problem in the beginning.

The following are suggestions for feeding your puppy when around the other dogs; this will reduce the chance of territorial behavior:

- Feed your Schnoodle at the same time as the other dogs but in a different room. Keeping them separated will let your Schnoodle eat without distractions or feeling that your other dogs will eat what is in his bowl. Make sure to feed your Schnoodle in the same room each time while the other dogs eat in their established areas.

- Keep your Schnoodle and other dogs in their areas until they finish eating their food. Some dogs have a tendency to leave food in the bowl. Don't let them. They need to finish everything in the bowl because all food bowls will be removed as soon as the dogs finish eating.

- Make sure you have someone near your Schnoodle so that he learns not to growl at people near his bowl. This will help reduce stress when other dogs are around the food. If your dog demonstrates any aggression, immediately correct him by saying, ""No," then give him praise when he stops. Do not play with the food bowl and make sure none of the kids play with it. Your dog needs to know that no one is going to try to steal his food.

- Over the course of a couple weeks, move your dogs closer together while eating. For example, you can feed your current dog on one side of the door near the doorway and the Schnoodle on the opposite side.

- After a month or two, you can feed the dogs in the same room but with some distance between them. If your Schnoodle starts to exhibit protective behavior with the other dogs, correct him, then praise him when he stops the behavior.

Eventually, you can start feeding the dogs close to one another. This can take weeks to months to accomplish depending on the age of the Schnoodle. A puppy will need less time because he will be socialized with the dogs from an early age, making him less wary. That does not mean he won't display territorial behavior. Yet, it likely won't take long for him to start to feel comfortable eating near the rest of the pack.

For adult dogs, this process could take longer, and you should not rush. Let your dog learn to feel comfortable eating before you make changes, even small ones. Dogs of any breed can be protective of their food depending on their past history, and this is exacerbated in protective breeds like the Schnoodle. Before your dog will eat peacefully, he must be assured that his protective behavior is not necessary around other dogs. That means letting his confidence and his comfort-level build at his own pace.

CHAPTER 8
The First Few Weeks

"I think the owner that has a plan in place for a training schedule does the best. Those first few months that you invest in your new puppy will pay off HUGE in the long run of their life!"

CATHERINE WILSON
Oodles of Schnoodles

Photo Courtesy of Sue Mitgang

A Schnoodle's intellect often shows as curiosity, and that means you are going to need to keep an eye on your pup. When he is not sleeping, you are going to have your hands full, but it will also be a lot of fun! The bond you start to build in the first week will continue to develop over the first month. By the end of the first month, your pup should be sleeping through the night and may

CELEBRITY SCHNOODLES
Weegee Danes

Clare Danes, American Actress and recipient of three Emmys, four Golden Globes, and two Screen Actors Guild Awards, is the proud owner of a Schnoodle named Weegee. Weegee lives with Danes and her husband, Hugh Dancy, at a country home in New York.

have a fairly good understanding of where to go to the bathroom. You will better understand your Schnoodle's personality, which will make it much easier to comfort your puppy during occasional bouts of uncertainty.

The first month is when you really need to start paying attention to your puppy's emerging personality. As with all intelligent breeds, the key is to remain consistent when it comes to training. That means everyone should be consistent, not just the person who is your dog's favorite. Always use what you learn about your puppy's personality to encourage good behavior!

Setting The Rules And Sticking To Them

Your puppy needs to understand the rules and to know you and your family mean them. Both parent breeds are intelligent, and they can be headstrong and willful. Once your canine learns to follow your commands, there will still be times when he will refuse to listen. However, he will be much more likely to listen when he knows you are in control. Schnoodles can be stubborn! No matter how cute your Schnoodle is, for your sake and his, you need to let him know you are the boss - in a firm but non-threatening manner.

Establish A No-Jumping And No-Mouthing Policy

If not properly trained, a Schnoodle that is afraid might possibly nip little children. This is potentially a problem with smaller breeds of Schnoodle because of their miniature Schnauzer tendencies. You have the responsibility to ensure that your dog learns how to play properly, which means no

Photo Courtesy
of Ali & David Rubenstein

jumping on people or nipping them. Any games that involve biting or nipping should always be avoided.

Nipping

- One of the triggers for nipping is overstimulation. This can be one sign your puppy is too tired to keep playing or training, and you should put him to bed.
- Another trigger could be your canine has too much energy. If this is the case, take your puppy outside to burn-off some of his excess energy. At the same time, be careful not to over-exercise the puppy.

You need to be vigilant and immediately let your puppy know nipping is not acceptable. Some people recommend using a water spritzer bottle and spraying the puppy while saying, "No," after nipping. This is one of the few times when punishment may be effective. Remember – make sure your dog does not associate the spraying with anything other than his nipping.

Always firmly tell your puppy, "No," whenever he is nipping even if it is during playtime. You should also pull away and loudly say, "Ouch!" to let your puppy know his teeth are hurting you. This will help to establish the idea that nipping is bad and is never rewarded.

Chewing

All puppies chew to relieve the pain of teething. Whether your dog is chewing your furniture, utensils, or clothing, be sure to discourage this behavior as quickly as possible:

- Make sure you have toys for your Schnoodle (whether an adult or a puppy) so you can teach him what objects are acceptable for chewing. Having a lot of available toys and rotating those toys out will give your puppy or dog several options.
- If your puppy is teething, either refrigerate a couple of toys so they are cold or give your puppy frozen carrots. The cold will help to numb the pain.
- Toys that are made either of hard rubber or hard nylon are best, particularly Kongs with kibble in them. You can even fill them with water and freeze them, which will give your puppy something cool to soothe the pain of teething.

For the most part, keeping an eye on your dog when he is not in his designated space will help you quickly see when he is chewing on things he shouldn't. When this happens, firmly say, "No." If your dog continues to chew, put him back in his space. While he is in the space, make sure he has plenty of toys to chew on.

If you decide to use chew deterrents, such as bitter training sprays, be aware some dogs will not care if an item tastes bad – they will chew it anyway. If you apply these deterrents, do not leave your dog alone and expect him to stop chewing. You should watch your dog's reaction before trusting that the bad habit is broken. Since some Schnoodles have separation anxiety, you should eliminate the chewing problem as quickly as possible; this will allow your pup to roam freely around your home.

Jumping

Dogs typically jump on people when they first greet them. Use the following steps when you have a visitor (and if you can get someone who is willing to help because that will make the training that much easier):

*Photo Courtesy
of Maureen Lemmon*

1. Put a leash on the dog when the person knocks on the door or rings the bell. The arrival of someone will invariably excite most dogs, especially puppies.

2. Let the person in, but do not approach the person with the puppy until your pup calms down.

3. Be effusive in your praise when the puppy keeps all four paws on the ground. Approach the visitor only after your Schnoodle is calm.

4. If the puppy jumps on the visitor, they should turn their body and ignore him. Don't verbally correct him. To be completely ignored will be far more of a deterrent than any words you can say.

5. Give your dog something to hold in his mouth if he does not settle down. Sometimes dogs just need a task to reduce their excitement. A stuffed animal or ball are ideal for distraction even if your dog drops it.

6. At this point, the visitor can get low and pet your dog. Having someone on his level will make him feel like he is being included. It also lets him sniff their face, which is part of a proper greeting to a dog. If your visitor is willing to help, this acknowledgment can prevent your pup from further jumping since he already feels safe with the person who is at his level.

Attention Seeking And Barking

Like toddlers and young children, your Schnoodle will resort to any means of getting your attention even if that attention is negative. There can be different ways of acting out, like destroying something or barking. Since what he really wants is your attention, the best way to train him is by ignoring him when he acts out. If he is barking, don't acknowledge him. Once he stops barking, count to five, then praise him for the quiet. If he destroys items that he isn't meant to destroy, remove the items so he can do no harm.

Ignoring your dog is what works best when deterring attention-seeking behavior. As difficult as that may be, it is necessary to keep your puppy from learning how to push your buttons. After all, you do not want those behaviors to escalate when he is an adult. He will be able to do a lot more damage when he is older, and his voice will be a lot louder!

Of course, you don't want to completely eliminate barking since Schnoodles can make good watch dogs. You simply want to train him but not to bark for attention just because he is bored.

Reward-Based Training Vs Discipline-Based Training

With an intelligent breed like the Schnoodle, it is much more efficient to train your puppy using rewards than with punishments. This will be a particular challenge as puppies can be exuberant and are easily distracted. It is important to remember that your puppy is young, so you need to keep your temper and to learn when a break from training is needed.

The following lists several critical aspects you will need to address during the first month:

- Housetraining (Chapter 9)
- Crate training (Chapter 6)
- Barking (Chapter 11)

Find out how much housetraining was completed by the breeder. The best breeders may even teach puppies one or two commands before the puppy goes home with you. If this is the case, keep using those same commands with your puppy so the early training is not lost. This information can help you establish the right tone of voice to use with your puppy since he will already know what the words mean and how to react to them.

Separation Anxiety In Dogs And Puppies

Poodles are usually considered breeds with substantial separation anxiety, but Schnauzers do not show the same anxiety. Standard Poodles may not be quite as bad as the smaller breeds, but all working dogs are more likely to have separation anxiety. Working-dog separation anxiety is a bit different than toy-breed anxiety. If you give your working dog something to do while you are gone, the separation won't be quite so intense; he will mostly just get bored. Still, it is a problem that you are likely to encounter, so you need to help your puppy understand that your leaving the house doesn't mean you won't return.

Schnoodles are not known for being prone to separation anxiety, probably because they are more independent dogs. However, that doesn't mean it is a guarantee your dog will always be fine. If your Schnoodle does have separation anxiety, he can do a lot of damage when left alone. Besides tiring out your dog before leaving home, there are other ways you can prepare your puppy or dog for long days when he is home alone.

In the beginning, keep the puppy's time alone to a minimum. The sounds of people moving around the house will help your Schnoodle understand the separation is not permanent. After the first week or so, alone time can involve you going out to get the mail, leaving the puppy inside by himself for just a few minutes. You can then lengthen the amount of time you are away from the puppy until he is alone for thirty minutes or so at a time.

The following are some basic guidelines for when you begin to leave your puppy alone:

- Take the puppy outside about thirty minutes before you leave.
- Tire the puppy out with exercise or playtime so that your leaving is not such a big deal.
- Place him in his puppy area - well ahead of when you plan on leaving - to avoid him associating his space with something bad.
- Don't give your puppy extra attention right before you leave. This only reinforces the idea you give attention before something bad happens.
- Avoid reprimanding your Schnoodle for any bad behavior that happens while you are away. Reprimanding teaches him to be more stressed because it will seem like you come home angry.

The following is a list of actions you can take to comfort your dog if you see signs of separation anxiety:

Photo Courtesy of Cynthia Gaddis

- Chew toys can give your dog something acceptable to gnaw on while you are away.
- A blanket or shirt that smells like you or other family members can help provide comfort, too. This is an ideal strategy if you have previously worn the item. (Make sure you were not in contact with any chemicals the day you wore it.) Consider giving the dog something you know you won't wear again in case he shreds it to pieces.
- Leave the puppy's area well-lit even if it is during the day. Should something happen and you get home later than you intended, you don't want your little guy to be in the dark.
- Turn on a classical music radio station or a quiet television program – like Mr. Ed or I Love Lucy. Your goal is to prevent the house from being completely quiet where unfamiliar noises are obvious.

It will not take your Schnoodle long to notice the behaviors that mean you will be leaving soon. Grabbing your keys, purse, or wallet will become triggers that might make your Schnoodle anxious. Don't make a big deal out of it. If you act in a normal way, over time this will help your little one understand that your leaving is fine and that everything will be all right.

How Long Is Too Long To Be Left Home Alone?

In the beginning, your dog should spend only a brief period of time in the crate while you are gone. You should not leave him alone for more than eight hours. He will likely be all right by himself between four and eight hours, but any longer than that and he may start to have problems. Though the breed is often independent, they are still pack animals. They do better when they have their pack than when they are left home alone for lengthy periods of time.

As your dog becomes housetrained and trustworthy, you should allow him to leave the crate while you are gone so he doesn't feel he is being punished. Your new companion will not do well trapped in a crate for hours at a time!

You also need to find some good mental games that will keep your pup occupied while you are gone. Whether you bring home a puppy or an adult Schnoodle, it is vital that your home is "dog-proofed" before your dog's arrival. You will be glad you removed those tempting objects when your dog is crate-trained, and you leave him alone for extended periods of time.

Don't Overdo It – Physically Or Mentally

As an adult, your Schnoodle will probably be a highly active dog. As a puppy, your Schnoodle will go from sleeping to being rambunctious to sleeping again all within a brief period of time. A tired puppy is a lot like a tired toddler; you have to keep the little guy from becoming exhausted or from overworking those little legs. You need to be careful about harming your puppy's growing bones. Your pup is probably going to think that sleep is unnecessary, no matter how tired he is. It is up to you to read the signs that tell you when to stop all activities and to take a break or to put your pup to bed.

You should train your dog in increments of time - only which he can handle. Don't push your puppy's training past his concentration level, and don't discourage your adult dog by using commands that are too advanced. If you continue training your puppy past his energy levels, the lessons learned are not going to be the ones you want to teach your dog. At this age, training sessions don't need to be long; they just need to be consistent.

Walks will be much shorter during the first month. When you go outside, stay within a few blocks of home. Don't worry – by the month's end, your puppy will have more stamina, so you can enjoy longer walks with your new friend. You can also do a bit of walking on the leash in the yard if your puppy has lots of extra energy. Puppies have a tendency to attack their leash while walking because it is a distraction from running freely. Taking walks will also help your Schnoodle learn how to behave on the leash.

Just because your puppy can't endure long walks initially doesn't mean he won't have plenty of energy. Daily exercise will be essential, with the caveat that you need to make sure your puppy isn't doing too much, too soon. Staying active will not only keep him healthy, but it will also keep him mentally stimulated. You will quickly realize how sedentary your "non-puppy life" has been because you will be on the move the entire time your puppy is awake!

CHAPTER 9
Housetraining

Housetraining a puppy is no more difficult or time consuming than potty training a toddler. It is important to set a schedule and to stick to it - no deviation!

Using a leash can help show your puppy where and when to go to the bathroom. However, there will still be challenges as you try to convince your puppy the designated place for the bathroom is not inside your home!

*Photo Courtesy
of Ali & David Rubenstein*

The following is a list of rules to apply when housetraining:

- Never let the puppy roam the house alone – he should always be in his dedicated puppy space when you are not watching him. Your Schnoodle won't like a soiled crate, so being in his crate is a deterrent from not doing his business there when you are not around. He may not feel the same approach about other areas of the home if he is free to wander.

- Give your puppy constant, easy access to the locations where you plan to housetrain him. You will need to make frequent trips outside with your puppy as he learns where to do his business. This can cause a problem if constant access to the restroom isn't always possible. When you go outside, put a leash on your puppy to make a point of where in the yard you want him to use the bathroom.

Always begin with a training plan; then, be even stricter with yourself than you are with your puppy when keeping the schedule. You are the key to your puppy's learning!

Inside Or Outside – Housetraining Options And Considerations

"I recommend to my puppy parents to use the 'bell method' of training to go out. Schnoodles are so very smart they usually pick up on this within a few days, if the parents are consistent! This method is basically training your new baby to have a way of communicating with you. It works amazingly!"

CATHERINE WILSON
Oodles of Schnoodles

If your breeder already started the housetraining process, make sure to coordinate your training so you pick up where they left off. Without a break in the training, your Schnoodle will housetrain faster than most dogs.

The following is a list of housetraining options for your puppy:

- Pee pads – You should have several around the home for training, including in the puppy's area, but as far from his bed as possible.

- Regular outings outside – Organize these outings based on your puppy's sleeping and eating schedule.

- Rewards – You can use treats in the beginning but quickly shift to praise.

Setting A Schedule

You need to keep an eye on your puppy and consistently have house-training sessions:

- After eating
- After waking up from sleeping or napping
- Follow a schedule (after it has been established)

One of the most important things you should watch for are cues - like sniffing and circling, which are two common signs a puppy exhibits when searching for a place to go. Start tailoring your schedule around your puppy's unique needs.

Puppies have small bladders and little control in the early days. If you train your pup to do his business inside, you need a designated space in the puppy's area for a clean pee pad. Make sure you change the pads regularly, so your puppy does not get accustomed to having waste nearby. Pee pads are better than newspaper and can absorb more. Even if you use pee pads, you should plan to transition your dog to do his business outdoors as quickly as possible.

Choosing A Location

A designated bathroom space will make the housetraining experience easier because your Schnoodle will associate one area of the yard for that specific purpose. Instead of sniffing around until he finds a choice spot, using one spot every time will also make cleanup simpler, and you will be able to use the entire yard instead of having to worry about stepping in waste. Given how much Schnoodles love to dig, you should definitely place the designated bathroom area away from any fences.

Schnoodles can be very particular about weather, so keeping the designated area close to the door and under some kind of protection will help during inclement weather.

The perfect time to train your puppy to go to the bathroom is when you go out for walks. Between walks and

SCHNOODLES IN BOOKS

Dog Sitters: A Man, A Woman, and A Schnoodle

In the novel *Dog Sitters* by Rozsa Gaston, the search for a missing Schnoodle is the daunting task for Hint Daniels and Jack Whitby. Will the duo resolve their differences and agree on a plan to find the runaway dog? And what will the mischievous Schnoodle get up to before he is found?

Photo Courtesy
of Tyler and Julie Hounsome

using the yard, your puppy will come to see the leash as a sign that it is time to relieve his bladder, which could become a Pavlovian response.

Do not send your puppy outside alone and assume he has done what you wanted him to do. He needs to understand the purpose of going outside is to go to the bathroom. Until there are no more accidents in the house, you need to be sure your puppy is not losing focus.

Keyword Training

All training should include keywords, even housetraining. You and all family members should consistently use these keywords when housetraining your dog. If you have paired an adult with a child, the adult should be the one using the keyword during training.

To avoid confusing your puppy, be careful not to select words that you often use inside the home. Use a phrase like, "Get busy," to let your puppy know it's time to go outside to do his business. Do not use words like "bathroom" or "potty" because these words are used in casual conversation, which could trigger a desire to go to the bathroom. "Get busy" is not a phrase most people use in their daily routine, so it is not something you are likely to say unless you want your puppy to go to the bathroom outside. This would be a great keyword.

Once your puppy learns to use the bathroom based on the command, make sure he finishes before offering praise or rewards.

Reward Good Behavior With Positive Reinforcement

Positive reinforcement is highly effective. In the beginning, take a few pieces of kibble with you when you are teaching your puppy where to go, both inside and outside the home. Learning you are the one in charge will help teach your Schnoodle to look to you for cues and instructions.

Part of being consistent with training means lavishing the little guy with praise whenever your puppy does the right thing. Use a leash to gently lead your puppy to his bathroom area with no stops between. It will gradually become obvious to your Schnoodle this is where he should go to use the bathroom. Once you get outside, encourage your pup to go only when you get to the place in the yard that is intended for his bathroom spot. As soon as

Photo Courtesy of Koreen Hirakami

he does his business, give him immediate and very enthusiastic praise. Pet your puppy as you talk and let the little guy know just how good the action was. Once the praise is done, return inside immediately. This is not playtime. You want your puppy to associate certain outings with designated potty time.

While praise is far more effective for Schnoodles, you can also give your puppy a treat after a few successful trips outside. Definitely do not make treats a habit after each trip because you do not want your Schnoodle to expect one every time he does his business. The lesson is to go outside, not to receive a treat every time.

The best way to housetrain in the first couple of months is to go out every hour or two, even during the night. You will need to set an alarm to wake yourself during the night, so you remember to take the puppy

83

outside. Use the leash to keep the focus on using the bathroom, give the same enthusiastic praise, then immediately return inside and go to bed. It is difficult, but your Schnoodle will get the hang of it a lot faster if there isn't a lengthy period between potty breaks. Over time, the pup will need to go outside less frequently.

Cleaning Up

A dog's ability to smell things that humans can't smell creates a problem when it comes to accidents inside the home. Once a dog goes to the bathroom in your home, that smell will remain there for other dogs to smell.

This means you have to be very diligent about handling accidents:

- Clean up any messes in the house as soon as you find them.
- In areas where your dog has an accident, you should thoroughly clean the spot so there is no remaining scent. Your Schnoodle might take any lingering odor as a sign that the spot is an acceptable place to use the bathroom.

Spend a bit of time researching what kinds of cleaner you want to use, whether generic or holistic. For example, you will likely want to get a product with an enzyme cleaner. Enzymes help to remove stains by speeding up the chemical reaction of the cleaner with the stain. They also help to remove the smell faster, which reduces the odds your dog will continue to go to the bathroom in the same place. If Schnoodles are properly trained, they feel no need to mark their territory, but you should also discourage other dogs from claiming areas around your property.

If your Schnoodle has an accident, it is important to refrain from punishing the puppy. Punishment simply teaches your dog to hide his mess or to be stealthier about when he goes inside. Accidents are not a reason to punish – if they happen often, it is really more of a reflection of your training and your schedule than on the puppy. However, even the best trainers can tell you accidents are pretty much an inevitability. When it happens, tell your puppy, "No! Potty outside!" and clean up the mess immediately. Once you have finished cleaning the mess, take the puppy outside to go potty. It isn't likely that he will need to potty again, but it is worth the attempt in case he still has a little left.

Pay attention to when these accidents happen and determine if there is a commonality between them. Perhaps you need to add an extra trip outside during the day for your puppy, or you should make a change in his walking schedule. Maybe there is something that is startling your dog and causing an accident.

CHAPTER 10
Socialization

"I advise my new puppy parents that the more time and energy they pour into their new Schnoodle in the first couple of months, as far as training and socialization goes, the better off they will be. It will pay off in spades in the life of your puppy because you are laying an amazing foundation!"

CATHERINE WILSON
Oodles of Schnoodles

When not properly socialized, Schnoodles can suffer from anxiety, which may make them more aggressive toward other dogs. Also, a poorly socialized Schnoodle is more likely to escape, even if that seems counterintuitive. You want your Schnoodle to be happy around other people and dogs and to learn the vast majority of them are not a threat to you or to your home.

Socialization allows your puppy to learn that playing with people inside your home or with dogs you encounter on your walks can be a lot of fun. To make sure your Schnoodle is comfortable, introduce socialization skills at an early age. This is even more critical for smaller Schnoodles as they tend to be more aggressive and vocal when they don't trust someone.

Remember that your puppy will need to have all his vaccinations before exposure to other dogs.

Socialization Can Make Life Easier In The Long Run

All dogs need socialization. Intelligent breeds are quite analytical; they should learn as early as possible that the world is usually a safe place and most people and animals do not pose a threat. It will also teach your puppy that acting in a dominant, aggressive way is not acceptable.

Another benefit of early socialization is that it can make life much more enjoyable for everyone involved, no matter what the situation. A socialized dog will approach the world from a much better place than a dog that is not socialized.

SCHNOODLES IN BOOKS
Layla's Rules

Layla's Rules: Five Rules All Schnoodles Know is a novel written by Dan Lucas and illustrated by Fernando Caretta. This story about adoption, acceptance, and family is told by Layla, the family Schnoodle. The book was published by Brookline Booksmith in Brookline, Massachusetts, in 2015.

Greeting New People

Puppies will likely enjoy meeting new people, so make sure to invite friends over to help socialize your canine family member.

The following is a list of methods to use when introducing your puppy to a new person:

- Try to have your puppy meet new people daily, if possible. This could be during walks or while you are doing other activities, both in and out of the house. If you can't meet new people daily, try for at least four times a week.

- Invite friends and family over and let them spend a few minutes giving the puppy their undivided attention. If your puppy has a favorite game or activity, let people know so they can play with him. This will win the little guy over very quickly and teach him new people are fun and safe to be around.

- Once your puppy is old enough to learn to do tricks (after the first month), have your little friend perform his tricks for visitors.

- Avoid crowds for the first few months. When your puppy is older, attend dog-friendly events so your pup can learn to be comfortable around a large group of people.

Greeting New Dogs

Chapter 7 explained how to introduce your new Schnoodle to your other dogs. However, meeting dogs that are not part of your home is a little different, especially since you may encounter them at any time when you are out walking. The goal is to be able to walk around your neighborhood while your dog remains calm. Therefore, you need to train your Schnoodle as early as possible.

Most dogs will bow and sniff each other during an introduction. Remember to watch for signs of aggression (Chapter 7), such as raised hackles and bared teeth. Bowing, high tail, and perked ears usually mean that your Schnoodle is excited about meeting the other dog. If your Schnoodle is making noises, watch for signs of aggression to make sure that the sounds are playful and easy.

The best way to help a Schnoodle feel comfortable around unfamiliar dogs is to set up playdates with other dogs in a neutral place. This practice

Photo Courtesy
of Tricia Korth

Photo Courtesy of Koreen Hirakami

will allow your Schnoodle to meet a dog that is already known to be friendly. A playdate will also address territorial behavior or jealousy over sharing toys. This should make the whole experience much easier and with minimal issues.

Don't let your Schnoodle jump up on other dogs. If he does, immediately say, "No," to let him know it is not acceptable behavior. This action can become a way of showing dominance, which you really don't want with your puppy, even if it is just play in the beginning.

The Importance Of Continuing Socialization

Even friendly dogs need socialization, but this does not mean your puppy should be forced to interact with other dogs. However, joining classes and setting up playdates will give your dog a reason for excitement when meeting other dogs.

When family and friends visit, encourage them to bring their dogs. This will remind your Schnoodle his home is a welcoming place and not somewhere he needs to exert his dominance. You do not want your pup to think he can be a terror in his own house.

Socializing An Adult Dog

Socializing an adult canine requires a lot of time, dedication, gentle training, and a firm approach. You may be lucky enough to get an adult that is already well-socialized. That does not mean you can remain entirely relaxed! Your new dog may have had a terrible experience with a particular breed of dog that no one knows about, and this can result in a terrible situation.

Your dog should be adept at the following commands before you work on socialization:

- Sit
- Down
- Heel
- Stay

"Stay" is especially important because this demonstrates your dog has self-control by remaining in one place based on your command. This quality will be helpful when socializing because using this command will allow you to control him in any aggressive situation. When you go outside, you will need to be very aware of your surroundings and to be able to command your dog before another dog or person gets near.

- Use a short leash on walks. Being aware of your surroundings will start to cue you in regarding what is making your dog react, so you can start training your dog not to react negatively.

- Change direction if you notice your Schnoodle is not reacting well to a person or dog that is approaching. Avoidance is a good, short-term solution until you know your dog is more accepting of the presence of these other dogs or people.

- If you are not able to take a different direction, tell your dog to sit, then block your dog's view. This can prove to be particularly challenging as he will try to look around you. Continue to distract your dog so he will listen to you, taking his mind off what is coming toward him.

- Ask friends with friendly dogs to visit you then meet in an enclosed space. Having one or two friendly dogs to interact with can help your Schnoodle realize not all dogs are dangerous or need to be put in their place. When the dogs wander around the area together, with no real interaction, your dog will learn the others are enjoying the outside, too. So, there is no reason to try to bully them!

- Get special treats for when you go walking. If your dog is aggressive when walking, have him sit, and give him one of the special treats. Schnoodles are food motivated, so this could be a perfect way of distracting your dog from whatever is making him feel protective. At the first snarl or sign of aggression, engage the training mentality and draw upon your dog's desire for those special treats. This method is slow, but it is reliable because your dog will learn the appearance of strangers and other dogs means special treats for him. He will realize going on a walk is a positive experience, not a negative one. Nonetheless, this does not train him to interact with those dogs. Couple this tip with the fourth suggestion to get the best results.

If you have problems with your adult dog, consult a behaviorist or specialized trainer.

Photo Courtesy of Theresa Schornack

CHAPTER 11
Training Your Schnoodle

"This breed is so amazingly smart! They are a thinking breed! I am not sure there is a task or job that they could not be trained for. They are amazing service dogs in all capacities. They can do anything from obedience, to agility, to search and rescue, to just being an amazing family dog that can be taught all kinds of fun tricks! Expect an amazing dog that loves to please you and therefore is easy and a pleasure to train!"

CATHERINE WILSON
Oodles of Schnoodles

Photo Courtesy of Julie Johnson

By watching training videos of Aussiedoodles (a designer breed of Australian Shepherds and Poodles) you will also see your puppy's training capability. Ke ep that potential in mind during training sessions to keep frustration in check! The important thing is to make training fun. That said, you still have to be firm and consistent. Any training commands you teach during a training session should be used outside of the session, too.

Each training session is likely to leave you feeling pretty tired! Puppies simply cannot focus the way adult dogs can. There are just too many distractions. By making sure to follow through with a few actions, you will find your Schnoodle will pick up on the training much quicker. He will love the attention, but there may be times when your dog also just doesn't feel like listening. Giving him another treat will not do the trick so be careful about how many treats you hand out. (Another reason for restraint is the risk of your dog becoming overweight or obese.)

FUN FACT
Therapy Dogs

Due to their affectionate temperament and intelligence, Schnoodles are often trained as therapy dogs. This breed is known for being comfortable with strangers and easily trainable, making them ideal dogs for this line of work.

While training will become enjoyable over time, it will likely be slow going in the beginning as your dog will be quite excited for the interaction. You will need to be firm and consistent, as well as keeping the training sessions short in the beginning. If you are patient with your pup from the start, you will find it will pay off later.

Benefits Of Proper Training

In addition to making socialization and general excursions easier, training could be a way of saving your dog's life. Understanding commands might prevent your dog from running into the street, from responding to provocations from other dogs, or from acting as the aggressor.

Training is also a wonderful way to bond with your dog. This dedicated time together helps you understand your puppy's developing personality. It also allows you to learn what kind of reward will work best for other tasks, like socialization. Be sure your Schnoodle is well-trained so you can enjoy a full range of activities together - from picnics to outings in the park!

Choosing The Right Reward

The right reward for a Schnoodle will ultimately be love and affection. Treats are the easiest way of keying a puppy into the idea that performing tricks is a good behavior. Soon, though, you will need to switch to a reward that is a secondary reinforcer. Praise, additional playtime, and extra petting are all fantastic rewards for your Schnoodle. Your dog will probably follow you around until you decide to just sit back and relax. Plopping down to watch a movie and letting your puppy sit with you is a great reward after an intense training session. Not only did your puppy learn, but you both now get to relax together.

Remember, this is a breed that is prone to obesity, which can be detrimental to your dog's health. Make sure you switch to a different kind of positive reward as early as possible. Schnoodles love their toys, too, so don't rely solely on treats as a method of praise.

If you would like your Schnoodle to connect positive feedback with a sound, you can use a clicker. They are relatively inexpensive and should be used at the same time as you praise your puppy or dog. Clickers are not necessary, but some trainers find them useful.

Photo Courtesy
of Maureen Lemmon

Name Recognition

Over time, many of us create different names for our dogs. Nicknames, joke names, and descriptions based on some of their ridiculous actions can all be used later. However, before you can train a dog, you have to make sure he understands his real name.

The following list gives some name recognition suggestions:

1. Get some treats and show one to your dog.
2. Say the dog's name and immediately say, "Yes." (Your dog should be looking at you when you speak.) Then, give your dog a treat.
3. Wait ten seconds, then show your dog a treat and repeat step two.

Sessions shouldn't last longer than about five minutes because your dog will lose focus or interest. Name recognition is something you can do several times each day. After you have done this for five to ten sessions, the training will change a bit:

1. Wait until your dog isn't paying attention to you.
2. Call your dog. If he has a leash on, give it a gentle tug to get your dog's attention.
3. Say, "Yes," and give the dog a treat when he looks at you.

During this time, do not speak your dog's name when you correct him or for any reason other than the name recognition. This is because in the beginning, you need to get the dog to associate his name only with something positive, like treats. This will more quickly program your dog to listen to you no matter what else is going on around him.

It is likely your Schnoodle will not require a lot of time before he recognizes his name.

Essential Commands

There are five basic commands that all dogs should know. These commands are the basis for a happy and enjoyable relationship with your dog.

Train your puppy to do the commands in the order they appear in this chapter. Sit is a basic command and something all dogs naturally do. Since dogs sit often, it is the easiest command to teach. Teaching Leave It and Drop It is much more difficult, and it usually requires the puppy to fight an instinct or a desire. Consider how much you give in to something you want... when you know you shouldn't! That's pretty much what your puppy is facing. Quiet can be another difficult command as dogs (particularly puppies) tend to bark in response to their surroundings – with Schnoodles this is certainly not going to be a problem.

The following are some basic steps to use during training:

1. Include everyone in the home in the Schnoodle training. The puppy must learn to listen to everyone in the household and not just one or two people. A set training schedule may only involve a couple of people in the beginning, especially if you have children. There should always be an adult present when training but including a child will help reinforce the idea the puppy must listen to everyone in the house. It is also an effective way for a parent to monitor a child's interaction with the puppy so that everyone plays in a way that is safe and that follows the rules.

2. To get started, select an area where you and your puppy have no other distractions, including noise. Leave your phone and other devices out of range so you are able to keep your attention on the puppy.

3. Stay happy and excited about the training. Your puppy will pick up on your enthusiasm and will focus better because of it.

4. Be consistent and firm as you teach.

5. Bring a special treat to the first few training sessions, such as pieces of chicken or small treats.

Sit

Start to teach the command Sit when your puppy is around eight weeks old. Once you settle into your quiet training location:

1. Hold out a treat.

2. Move the treat over your puppy's head. This will make the puppy move back.

3. Say, "Sit" as the puppy's haunches touch the floor.

Having a second person around to demonstrate this with your puppy will be helpful as they can sit to show what you mean.

Wait until your puppy starts to sit down and say, "Sit," as he sits. If your puppy finishes sitting down, give praise. Naturally, this will make your puppy excited and wiggly, so it may take a bit of time before he will want to sit again. When the time comes and the puppy starts to sit again, repeat the process.

It's going to take more than a couple of sessions for the puppy to fully connect your words with the actions. Commands are something completely new to your little companion. Once your puppy has demonstrated mastery of the command Sit, start teaching Down.

Down

Repeat the same process when teaching this command as you did for Sit:

1. Tell your dog to Sit.

2. Hold out the treat.

3. Lower the treat to the floor with your dog sniffing at it. Allow your pup to lick the treat, but if he stands up, start over.

4. Say, "Down," as the puppy's elbows touch the floor (make sure to say it as they do the action to help them associate the word with the action), then give praise while giving your puppy the treat.

It will probably take a little less time to teach this command. Wait until your puppy has mastered Down before moving on to Stay.

Stay

Stay is a vital command to teach because it can keep your puppy from running across a street or from running at someone who is nervous or scared of dogs. It is important your dog has mastered Sit and Down before you teach Stay. Learning this command is going to be more difficult since it is not something your puppy does naturally.

Be prepared for this command to take a bit longer:

1. Tell your puppy to either Sit or Stay.

2. As you do this, place your hand in front of the puppy's face.

3. Wait until the puppy stops trying to lick your hand before you begin again.

4. When the puppy settles down, take a step away. If your puppy is not moving say, "Stay," and give a treat and some praise.

Giving your puppy the reward indicates the command is over, but you also need to indicate the command is complete. The puppy has to learn to stay until you say it is okay to leave the spot. Once you give the okay to move, do not give treats. The command Come should not be used as the okay word as it is a command used for something else.

Repeat these steps, taking more steps further away from the puppy after a successful command.

Once your puppy understands Stay when you move away, start training him to Stay even if you are not moving. Extend the amount of time required for the puppy to stay in one spot so he understands Stay ends with the Okay command.

When you feel that your puppy has the command Stay mastered, start training the puppy to Come.

Come

This is a command you can't teach until the puppy has learned the previous commands. Before you start the training session, decide if you want to use Come or Come Here for the command. Be consistent in the words you use.

This command is important for the same reason as the previous one; if you are around people who are nervous around dogs, or if you encounter a wild animal or other distraction, this command will snap your puppy's attention back to you:

1. Leash the puppy.

2. Tell the puppy to Stay.

3. Move away from the puppy.

4. Say the command you will use for Come and give a gentle tug on the leash toward you.

Repeat these steps, building a larger distance between you and the puppy. Once the puppy seems to understand, remove the leash and start at a close distance. If your puppy doesn't seem to understand the command, give some visual clues about what you want. For example, you can pat your leg or snap your fingers. As soon as your puppy comes running over to you, offer a reward.

Off

This is different from training your dog not to jump on people (Chapter 8). This command is specifically to get your dog off furniture or surfaces that may be dangerous. This is training you will need to do on the fly because you are training your dog to stop an action. This means you have to react to that undesirable action. Having treats on hand will be essential when you see your dog getting up on things you don't want him to be on:

1. Wait for your dog to put his paws on something you don't want him on.

2. Say, "Off," and lure him away with a treat that you keep just out of his reach.

3. Say, "Yes," and give him a treat as soon as his paws are off the surface.

Repeat this every time you see the behavior. It will likely take at least half a dozen times before your dog understands he should not perform the action anymore. Over time, switch from treats to praise or playing with a toy.

Leave It

This is a difficult training command, but you need to train your dog to Leave It for when you are out on a walk and want him to ignore other people or dogs.

1. Let your dog see that you have treats in your hand, then close your hand. Your fist should be close enough for your dog to sniff the treat.

2. Say, "Leave it," when your dog starts to sniff your hand.

3. Say, "Yes," and give your dog a treat when he turns his head away from the treats. Initially, this will probably take a while as your dog will want those treats. Don't continue to say, "Leave it," as your dog should not be learning you will give a command more than once. You want him to learn he must do what you say the first time, which is why treats are recommended in the beginning. If a minute or more passes after giving the command, you can then issue it again, but make sure your canine is focused on you and not distracted.

These sessions should only last about five minutes. Your dog will need time to learn this command as you are teaching him to ignore something he does naturally. When he looks away and stops sniffing when you say, "Leave it," you can move on to more advanced versions of the training:

1. Leave your hand open so your dog can see the treats.

2. Say, "Leave it," when your dog starts to show interest. This will probably be immediately, since your hand will be open so be prepared.

   a. Close your fist if your dog continues to sniff or gets near the treats in your hand.

   b. Give your dog a treat from your other hand if he stops.

Repeat these steps until your dog finally stops trying to sniff the treats. When your dog seems to have this down, move on to the most difficult version of this command.

1. Place treats on the ground or let your dog see you hide them. Then, stay close to those treats.

2. Say, "Leave it," when your dog starts to show interest in sniffing the treats.

   a. Place a hand over the treats if he doesn't listen.

   b. Give a treat if your dog does listen.

From here, you can start training while standing further from the treat with your dog leashed, so you can stop him if needed. Then, start to use other things that your dog loves, such as a favorite toy or another tempting treat that you don't usually give him.

Drop It

This is going to be one of the most difficult commands you will teach your puppy because it goes against both your puppy's instincts and interests.

Your puppy wants to keep whatever he has, so you are going to have to offer him something better instead. It is essential to teach the command early though, as your Schnoodle could be very destructive in the early days. Furthermore, this command could save your pooch's life. When you are out for a walk, he will likely lunge at objects that look like food. However, with this command, he will drop anything he picks up.

Start with a toy and a treat, or a large treat that your dog cannot eat in a matter of seconds, such as a rawhide. Make sure the treat you have is one your puppy does not get very often so there is motivation to drop the toy or big treat.

1. Give your puppy the toy or large treat. If you want to use a clicker, too, pair it with the exciting treat you will use to help convince your puppy to drop the treat.

2. Show your puppy the exciting treat.

3. Say, "Drop it," and when he drops the treat or toy, tell him, "Good," and hand over the exciting treat while picking up the item.

4. Repeat this immediately after your puppy finishes eating the exciting treat.

You will need to keep reinforcing this command for months after it is learned because it is not a natural instinct. This is a time for an irresistible treat so your puppy is convinced to drop that cherished toy or the food he shouldn't be eating.

Quiet

Schnoodles are known for being a quiet breed, but if you have a puppy that tends to bark, you may want to train the pup not to bark too often. Initially, you can use treats sparingly to reinforce quiet if your pup enjoys making noise:

1. When your puppy barks for no obvious reason, tell him to be quiet and place a treat nearby. It is almost guaranteed your dog will fall silent to sniff the treat.

2. If your dog does fall silent say, "Good dog" or "Good quiet."

It will not take too long for your puppy to understand Quiet means no barking.

If you want your Schnoodle to be more of a watchdog, you will need to provide some guidance on when he should bark. A professional can help tailor the approach to training your dog when to bark at people at the door. Otherwise, you will want your dog to know he shouldn't be randomly barking at birds at the window or squirrels running around in the yard.

*Photo Courtesy
of Cindy Hood*

Where To Go From Here

Schnoodles are a breed that is fairly easy to train. However, this friendly breed with potentially wary behavior will benefit greatly from classes in the early days. Your dog will enjoy the extra socialization if you want to take him to a puppy or obedience class. Class is a safe environment and a wonderful opportunity for both of you to learn. Also, there will be an expert instructor present to show you the best way to teach your pup how to act.

For Schnoodles, you should have all training completed between three and six months. Until all commands are learned, it is best to avoid other types of advanced training. Between six and twelve months, you should be able to move to tricks, if your dog is willing to do them. Things like fetch and other games may be fun for your Schnoodle, especially if the pup learns to play when young. It is a good idea to train your Schnoodle to do some fun activities as they do get bored easily - all intelligent dog breeds do! Planning to do more fun activities around your home can help you keep your Schnoodle in shape and entertained.

Puppy Classes

Puppies can begin to go to puppy school as early as six weeks. This is the beginning of obedience training, but you need to be careful around other dogs until your puppy has completed his vaccinations. Talk with your vet about when is an appropriate time to begin classes or at least a safe time. Your vet may be able to recommend good puppy training classes in your area.

The primary purpose of these classes is socialization. Studies show one-third of all puppies have minimal exposure to unfamiliar people and dogs during the first twenty weeks of their life. This can make the outside world pretty scary! The puppy classes give you and your puppy a chance to learn how to meet and greet other people and dogs in a controlled environment. Dogs that attend these classes are much friendlier and are less stressed about such things as large trucks, loud noises, and unfamiliar visitors. They are also less likely to be nervous or suffer from separation anxiety.

This training is also good training for you! The same studies show owners who attended classes learned to react appropriately when their puppy was disobedient or misbehaved. The classes teach you how to train your puppy and how to deal with the emerging headstrong nature of your dog.

Many classes will help you with some of the basic commands, like Sit and Down. Look for a class that also focuses on socialization so that your puppy can get the most out of the instruction.

Obedience Training

After your puppy graduates from puppy school and understands most of the basic commands, you can switch to obedience classes. Some trainers offer at-home obedience training, but it is best to find a class so that your dog can continue practicing socialization. If your puppy attends puppy classes, the trainers there can recommend classes at the next level of training. Dogs of nearly any age can attend obedience training classes although your dog should be old enough to listen to commands before instruction begins.

Obedience training usually includes the following:

- Teaching or reinforcing basic commands, like Sit, Stay, Come, and Down.
- How to walk without pulling on the leash.
- How to properly greet people and dogs, including not jumping on them.

Obedience school is as much about training you as training your dog. It helps you learn how to train while getting your dog through basic commands and how to behave for basic tasks, like greetings and walking. Classes usually last between seven and ten weeks.

Ask your vet for recommendations and also consider the following when evaluating trainers:

- Are they certified, particularly the CPDT-KA certification?
- How many years have they been training dogs?
- Do they have experience with training Schnoodles?
- Can you participate in the training? If the answer is no, do not use that trainer. You have to be a part of your dog's training because the trainer won't be around for most of your dog's life.

Therefore, your dog has to learn to listen to you.

If your dog has anxiety, depression, or other serious behavioral problems, you need to hire a trainer to help your dog work through those issues. Do your research to be sure your trainer is an expert - preferably one with experience training intelligent, strong-willed dogs. If possible, find someone who has experience dealing with Schnoodles.

Once your Schnoodle understands the basic commands and has done well in obedience training, you will know if more difficult training is right for your him.

CHAPTER 12
Nutrition

"What you choose to feed is of the utmost importance! Do your research! I suggest no corn, wheat or soy at the minimum. Read the labels. Do a search and see how many times they have recalls of that food. Feel good about what you feed and your Schnoodle will feel good too!"

CATHERINE WILSON
Oodles of Schnoodles

Some Schnoodles are enthusiastic eaters (from the Poodle side) while others are less food driven (from the Schnauzer side). It is best to work under the assumption your pup will take after the Poodle side so be careful about over feeding your little guy. It is far too easy to give your dog too many treats, especially if everyone in your family "trains" the dog. If everyone becomes accustomed to training the dog with praise or toys instead of treats, your dog's weight and stomach will be less problematic. With bloat being a potential issue (covered in more detail in Chapter 16), you want to keep your Schnoodle happy and healthy.

Some Schnoodles also have food allergies, so a grain-free diet is recommended. (Keep this is mind if you don't want to read through the whole chapter.) One positive trait of a Schnoodle is both parents are refined eaters, so you aren't going to deal with excessive drooling or slobbering – at least no more than with other breeds.

Why A Healthy Diet Is Important

Just because your Schnoodle is active doesn't mean he is burning all the calories he takes in, especially if you have an open treat policy. Just as you should not be eating all day, your puppy shouldn't be either. If you have a busy schedule, it will be too easy for your dog to have substantial lapses in activity levels while you are home. Your Schnoodle isn't going to understand your schedule changes. He will only recognize his activity level has nothing to do with the amount of food going into his mouth. This means he is likely to gain weight when you keep the calories the same while reducing the activities.

You need to be aware of roughly how many calories your dog eats a day, including treats, so be mindful of your dog's weight and if he is putting on pounds. This will tell you if you should adjust his food intake or if you should change the food to something more nutritional and with fewer calories.

Always talk with your vet if you have concerns about your Schnoodle's weight.

Photo Courtesy of Renae Facundus

Dangerous Foods

Dogs can eat raw meat without having to worry about the kinds of problems a person would encounter. However, there are some human foods that could be fatal to your Schnoodle.

The following is list of foods you should NEVER feed your dog:

- Apple seeds
- Chocolate
- Coffee
- Cooked bones (They can kill a dog when the bones splinter in the dog's mouth or stomach.)
- Corn on the cob (The cob is deadly to dogs; corn off the cob is fine.)
- Grapes/raisins
- Macadamia nuts
- Onions and chives
- Peaches, persimmons, and plums
- Tobacco (Your Schnoodle will not realize it is not a food and may eat it if it's left out.)
- Xylitol (a sugar substitute in candies and baked goods)
- Yeast

In addition to this list, consult the Canine Journal for a lengthy list of other dangerous foods. (http://www.caninejournal.com/foods-not-to-feed-dog/)

Canine Nutrition

"I recommend you give your Schnoodle vitamin supplements. With any dog food nowadays you really do not know if they are getting everything they need just from the food, especially trace minerals."

ANGELA DENNY
Angela's Schnoodles

The dietary needs of a dog are significantly different from a human's needs. People are more omnivorous than dogs, meaning they require a wider range of nutrients to be healthy. Canines are largely carnivorous, and protein is a significant dietary need. However, they need more than just protein to be healthy.

The following table provides the primary nutritional requirements for dogs:

Nutrient	Sources	Puppy	Adult
Protein	Meat, eggs, soybeans, corn, wheat, peanut butter	22.0% of diet	18.0% of diet
Fats	Fish oil, flaxseed oil, canola oil, pork fat, poultry fat, safflower oil, sunflower oil, soybean oil	8.0 to 15.0% of diet	5.0 to 15.0% of diet
Calcium	Dairy, animal organ tissue, meats, legumes (typically beans)	1.0% of diet	0.6% of diet
Phosphorus	Meat and pet supplements	0.8% of diet	0.5% of diet
Sodium	Meat, eggs	0.3% of diet	0.06% of diet

The following are the remaining nutrients dogs require, all of them less than 1% of a puppy or an adult diet:

- Arginine
- Histidine
- Isoleucine
- Leucine
- Lysine
- Methionine + cystine
- Phenylalanine + tyrosine
- Threonine
- Tryptophan
- Valine
- Chloride

It is best to avoid giving your dog human foods with a lot of sodium and preservatives. Water is also absolutely essential to keep your dog healthy. There should always be water in your dog's water bowl so make a habit of checking it several times a day, so your dog does not get dehydrated.

Proteins And Amino Acids

Since dogs are carnivores, protein is one of the most important nutrients in a healthy dog's diet. (They should not eat meat nearly as much as their close wolf relatives. Dogs' diets and needs have changed significantly since they have become human companions.) Proteins contain the necessary amino acids for your dog to produce glucose, which is essential for giving your dog energy. A lack of protein in your dog's diet will result in him being lethargic. His coat may start to look dull, and he is likely to lose weight.

Conversely, if your dog gets too much protein, his body will store the excess protein as fat, and he will gain weight. Meat is the best source of protein for your dog, and since a dog's dietary needs are significantly different from a human's needs. Still, it is possible for a dog to have a vegetarian diet as long as you ensure your dog receives necessary protein from other sources. You will also need to include supplemental vitamin D in his food. If you plan to feed your dog a vegetarian diet, talk to your vet first. It is incredibly difficult to ensure that a carnivore receives adequate protein while on a vegetarian diet. This is especially true of puppies. If this is your choice, you will need to have discussions with nutrition experts and to do your research. It is vitally important that your dog receives the necessary proteins for his needs.

Fat And Fatty Acids

Most fats that your dog needs are also found in meat. Seed oils provide a lot of necessary healthy fats, too, with peanut butter being one of the most common sources. Fats break down into fatty acids, which your dog needs for fat-soluble vitamins that help with regular cell functions. Perhaps the most obvious benefit of fats and fatty acids can be seen in your dog's coat. Your dog's coat will look and feel much healthier when your dog is getting the right nutrients.

The following is a list of potential health issues that might arise if your dog does not get adequate fats in his daily diet:

- His coat will look less healthy.
- His skin may be dry and itchy.
- His immune system could be compromised, making it easier for your dog to get sick.
- He may have an increased risk of heart disease. The primary concern if your dog gets too much fat is he will become obese, leading to additional health problems. An estimated 18% of Schnoodles have heart problems.

Carbohydrates And Cooked Foods

Dogs have been living with humans for millennia, so their dietary needs have evolved like our own. They can eat foods with carbohydrates to supplement the energy typically provided by proteins and fats. If you cook grains (such as barley, corn, and rice) prior to feeding them to your dog, it will be easier for him to digest those complex carbohydrates.

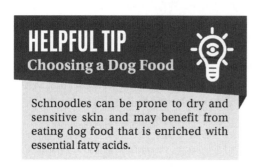

HELPFUL TIP
Choosing a Dog Food

Schnoodles can be prone to dry and sensitive skin and may benefit from eating dog food that is enriched with essential fatty acids.

Different Dietary Requirements For Different Life Stages

Different stages of a dog's life have different nutritional needs:
- Puppies
- Adults
- Senior dogs

Puppy Food

Dog food manufacturers produce a completely different type of food for puppies than for adult dogs. This is because their nutritional needs are much different than their adult counterparts. During roughly the first twelve months of their lives, puppies' bodies are growing. To be healthy, they need more calories and have different nutritional needs to promote growth. Puppies can have up to four meals a day, just be careful not to overfeed them, particularly if you use treats during training.

Adult Dog Food

The primary difference between puppy food and adult dog food is puppy food is higher in calories and nutrients which promote growth. Dog food manufacturers reduce these nutrients in adult dog food as they no longer need to sustain growth. As a rule, when a dog reaches about 90% of his predicted adult size, you should switch to adult dog food.

The size of your dog is key in determining how much to feed him. The following table is a general recommendation for daily food consumption for our adult Schnoodle. Initially, you may want to focus on the calories as you try to find the right balance for your dog.

Dog Size	Calories
10 lbs.	420 during hot months
	630 during cold months
20 lbs.	700 during hot months
	1,050 during cold months
30 lbs.	900 during hot months
	1,400 during cold months
50 lbs.	1,350 during hot months
	2,000 during cold months
70 lbs.	1,680 during hot months
	2,500 during cold months

Feeding your Schnoodle twice a day is recommended, so you can divide up the calories according to this schedule. Keep in mind these recommendations are per day and not per meal.

If you plan to add wet food, pay attention to the total calorie intake and adjust how much you feed your dog between the kibble and wet food. The total calories in the kibble and wet food should balance out so as not to exceed your dog's needs. The same is true if you give your dog a lot of treats over the course of the day. You should factor treat calories into how much you feed your dog at mealtimes.

If you feed your dog homemade food, you should learn your nutrition facts, and you should pay close attention to calories instead of cup measurements.

Senior Dog Food

Senior dogs are not always capable of being as active as they were in their younger days. If you notice your dog is slowing down or suffers joint pain and shows a lack of stamina when taking long walks, you can assume your dog is entering his senior years. Consult with your vet if you think it is time to change the type of food you feed him.

The primary difference between adult and senior dog food is senior dog food contains less fat and more antioxidants to help fight weight gain. Senior dogs also need more protein, which will probably make your dog happy because that usually means more meat and meat flavors. Protein helps to maintain your dog's aging muscles. He should also be eating less phosphorous during his golden years to avoid the risk of developing hyper-phosphatemia. This is a condition where dogs have excessive amounts of phosphorous in their bloodstream, and older dogs are at greater risk of developing it. The level of phosphorous in the body is controlled by the kidney; as such, elevated levels of phosphorous are usually an indication of a problem with the kidneys.

Senior dog food has the correct number of calories for reduced activity, which means no adjustment of quantity is needed unless you notice weight gain. Consult your vet if you notice your dog is putting on weight because this could be a sign of a senior dog ailment.

Your Dog's Meal Options

You have three primary choices for what to feed your dog, or you can use a combination of the three, depending on your situation and your dog's specific needs:

- Commercial food
- Raw diet
- Homemade diet

Commercial Food

Make sure that you are buying the best dog food you can afford. Take the time to research each of your options, particularly the nutritional value of the food, and review this annually. Make sure the food you are giving your dog is high quality, and always take into account your dog's size, energy levels, and age. Your puppy may not need puppy food for as long as other breeds and dog food for seniors may not be

The website Pawster provides several great articles about which commercial dog foods are best for Schnoodles. Since new foods frequently come on the market, check periodically to see if there are new, better foods that have become available.

If you aren't sure which brand of food is best, talk with the breeder about the foods they recommend. Breeders are really the best guides for you here, as they are experts, but you can also ask your vet.

Some dogs may be picky eaters who certainly get tired of repeatedly eating the same food. Just as you switch up your meals, you can also change what your Schnoodle eats. While you shouldn't frequently change the brand of food, you can get foods that have assorted flavors. You can also change

Photo Courtesy of Julie Johnson

the taste by adding a bit of wet (canned) food. Adding one-fourth to one-third of a can for each meal is an easy change to make for your dog's happiness.

For more details on commercial options, check out the website - Dog Food Advisor. They provide reviews on various dog food brands as well as providing information on recalls and contamination issues.

Commercial Dry Food

Dry dog food often comes in bags, and it is what the vast majority of people feed their dogs.

Dry Dog Food

PROS	CONS
• Convenience	• Requires research to ensure you don't buy doggie junk food
• Variety	• Packaging is not always honest
• Availability	• Recalls for food contamination
• Affordability	• Loose FDA nutritional regulations
• Manufacturers follow nutritional recommendations (not all of them follow this, so do your brand research before you buy)	• Low quality food may have questionable ingredients
• Specially formulated for different canine life stages	
• Can be used for training	
• Easy to store	

The convenience and ease on your budget mean you are almost certainly going to buy kibble for your dog, too. This is perfectly fine, and most dogs will be more than happy to eat kibble. Be sure you know what brand you are feeding your dog and pay attention to kibble recalls, so you can stop feeding your dog if necessary. Check out the following sites regularly to for recall information:
- Dog Food Recalls
- American Kennel Club
- Dog Food Guide

Commercial Wet Food

Most dogs prefer wet dog food over kibble, but it is also more expensive. Wet dog food can be purchased in larger packs that can be extremely easy to store.

Wet Dog Food

PROS	CONS
• Helps keep dogs hydrated	• Dog bowls must be washed after every meal
• Has a richer scent and flavor	• Can soften bowel movements
• Easier to eat for dogs with dental problems (particularly those missing teeth) or if a dog has been ill	• Can be messier than kibble
	• Once opened, it has a very short shelf life, and should be covered and refrigerated
• Convenient and easy to serve	• More expensive than dry dog food, and comes in small quantities
• Unopened, it can last between 1 and 3 years	• Packaging is not always honest
• Balanced based on current pet nutrition recommendations	• Recalls for food contamination
	• Loose FDA regulations

Like dry dog food, wet dog food is convenient, and picky dogs are much more likely to eat it than kibble. When your dog gets sick, use wet dog food to ensure that he is still eating and gets the necessary nutrition each day. It may be harder to switch back to kibble once your Schnoodle is healthy, but you can always add a little wet food to make each meal more appetizing.

Raw Diet

- For dogs prone to food allergies (like Schnoodles), raw diets can help prevent an allergic reaction to wheat and processed foods. Raw diets are heavy in raw meats, bones, vegetables, and specific supplements. Some of the benefits to a raw diet include:
- Improves your dog's coat and skin
- Improves immune system
- Improves health (as a result of better digestion)
- Increases energy
- Increases muscle mass

Raw diets are meant to give your dog the kind of food he ate before being domesticated. It means giving your dog uncooked meats, whole (uncooked) bones, and a bit of dairy products. It doesn't include any processed food of any kind – not even food cooked in your kitchen.

However, there are potential risks to this diet. Dogs have been domesticated for millennia, and their digestive system has also evolved. Trying to force them to eat the kind of diet they ate hundreds of years ago does not always work as intended. Primarily because they may not be able to fully digest raw food the way their ancestors did.

There are also many risks associated with feeding dogs uncooked meals, particularly if the food has been contaminated. Things like bacteria pose a serious risk and can be transferred to you if your dog gets sick. Many medical professionals also warn about the dangers of giving dogs bones even if they are uncooked. Bones can splinter in your dog's mouth and puncture the esophagus or stomach.

The Canine Journal provides a lot of information about a raw diet, including different recipes and how to transition your dog to this diet.

Homemade Diet

If you mix dog food from scratch (not with a microwave or a boxed meal), you will find it doesn't take much time to provide a healthy meal for your companion.

Keeping in mind the foods your Schnoodle absolutely should not eat, you can mix some of the food you make for yourself into your Schnoodle's meal. Just make sure to add a bit more of the nutrients your Schnoodle needs. Although you and your Schnoodle have distinctly different dietary needs, you can tailor both foods to include the same nutrients.

Do not feed your Schnoodle from your plate! Split the food, placing your dog's meal into a bowl so your canine understands your food is just for you. The best home-cooked meals should be planned in advance so your Schnoodle gets the correct nutritional balance.

Typically, 50% of your dog's food should be animal protein (fish, poultry, and organ meats). About 25% should be full of complex carbohydrates. The remaining 25% should be from fruits and vegetables, particularly foods like pumpkin, apples, bananas, and green beans. These foods provide extra flavor your Schnoodle will probably love, while filling him up faster and reducing the chance of overeating.

The following are a few sites where you can learn how to make homemade meals for canines. Some of them are not breed specific, so if you have more than one dog, these meals can be made for all your furry, canine friends:

- Homemade Dog Food with a Special Ingredient
- Dog Recipes Made from Scratch – Schnauzer Rules
- Homecooking for you Schnauzer
- Home Cooking for Poodles
- DIY Homemade Dog Food
- DORG Daily Diet
- Dogsaholic

Scheduling Meals

Your Schnoodle will likely expect you to stick to a schedule, which definitely includes mealtimes. If treats and snacks are something you establish as a normal routine, your dog will expect that, too!

For puppies, plan to have three or four meals, while adults and seniors should typically have two meals a day.

Food Allergies And Intolerance

Whenever you start your dog on a new type of food (even if it's simply a different flavor), you need to monitor him while he becomes accustomed to the change. Food allergies are fairly common in Schnoodles, and the symptoms manifest themselves as hot spots, which are similar to rashes in humans. Your dog may start scratching or chewing specific spots on his body, and his fur could start falling out around those spots.

Some dogs don't have individual hot spots, but the allergy shows up on their entire coat. If your Schnoodle seems to be shedding more fur than normal, take him to the vet to be checked for food allergies.

If you give your dog something his stomach cannot handle, it will probably be obvious when your dog is unable to hold his bowels. If he is already housetrained, he will probably either pant at you or whimper to let you know he needs to go outside. Get him outside as quickly as you can so he does not have an accident. Flatulence will also probably occur more often if your Schnoodle has a food intolerance.

Since the symptoms of food allergies and intolerances look similar to a reaction to nutritional deficiencies, you should visit your vet immediately! This is especially true if you notice any problems with your dog's coat or skin.

CHAPTER 13
Exercise Needs

Regardless of which breed your Schnoodle takes after, playfulness is very nearly guaranteed! Both Poodles and Schnauzers are loving and energetic dogs. This chapter covers games and activities you and your Schnoodle can enjoy while building his strengths and his natural abilities.

As a general rule, plan at least thirty minutes per day of solid exercise for smaller Schnoodles and an hour a day for larger dogs. On rainy days, it will be easy to exercise the energy out of a smaller dog! However, larger Schnoodles will be a bit trickier because they will need to be active for longer periods – in the rain!

It's also important to include some mental stimulation with all exercises and activities. An intelligent breed like your Schnoodle needs mental engagement to keep him from getting bored - another reason why tricks are a recommended activity. We all know a bored Schnoodle can be a destructive Schnoodle! Part of adopting an intelligent breed is accepting that you are going to need to ensure your dog is happily occupied.

Since Poodles are prone to separation anxiety, you would be wise to tire-out your pup before you leave the house. This will ensure that potentially destructive and nervous tendencies will be minimized.

Outdoor Activities

Your Schnoodle is going to love being out and about exploring the world! All outdoor activities will require more time and training than indoor activities, and the size of your Schnoodle will affect some aspects of play, too. Still, it is worth the effort to see your dog's eyes light-up during those special times!

Enjoyable Day Trips

With such a friendly, fun-loving dog, day trips will be loads of fun with your Schnoodle! Not only will he enjoy riding in the car with you, but he will also enjoy exploring the town, beach, or unfamiliar area you have chosen. (This has the added benefit of tiring out your Schnoodle for the next day - at least when he is six or seven years old.) Day trips are great bonding experiences, and it encourages you and your family to discover new and interesting locations!

*Photo Courtesy
of Jennifer Sturgeon*

You will need to bring water for your dog wherever you go. Your dog will need hydration during the trip...just like you. As far as temperatures are concerned, Schnoodles tend to tolerate hotter weather (but not too hot) more than other breeds. A good rule of thumb in chilly weather is if you need a coat, so does your Schnoodle!

A Fantastic Jogging And Swimming Companion

If you are looking for a great jogging companion, your Schnoodle will be the perfect partner! However, the size of your Schnoodle will dictate the length of your jog. If you have a smaller Schnoodle, a shorter, slower jog would be best; still, you could jog in the morning and again in the evening, which would really tire your pup! For larger Schnoodles, they will probably take a long jog in stride and put you to shame!

You should not jog with your Schnoodle during the first year or two of their lives because several considerations must first be met:

- Be sure your dog understands the 'Heel" command before you take him jogging.
- Jog on softer ground, such as dirt paths, as often as you can because you need to protect the pads of your Schnoodle's feet. Remember, he isn't wearing extra padding on his feet!
- Don't go for long runs in the beginning. Your Schnoodle needs to build his stamina and his understanding of the activity.

Many Schnoodles also love to swim. On days when you go to the lake, the beach, or any other body of water, you can take your dog and have a wonderful time! If you have a pool and want your dog to join you, there will probably be no arguments from your pup – maybe a face full of water as he splashes into the pool!

Swimming is a far more tiring activity than walking or jogging. Of course, there is always clean-up afterward so don't forget to take a couple of towels to dry off your Schnoodle. (You might also want to have your Schnoodle's coat cut before a swim to reduce how much water he absorbs.) If you do go swimming, make sure to thoroughly dry your Schnoodle so he doesn't get cold after all the fun.

Agility Training

Better known as an obstacle course, agility training is a fantastic way to keep your adult dog running and happy at the same time. When you guide your dog through the course, you will build a strong bond between the two of you, and this experience will allow your dog to feel more comfortable when outside the home. He will also learn he doesn't need to dominate

*Photo Courtesy
of Kally-Anna Clinton*

everyone in the area. Since you will be the one in control, your dog will likely be confused in the beginning so be prepared for the two of you to look a bit silly at first. The point is to have fun and to keep your dog engaged so securing and holding his attention is key to being successful.

Two to three hours a week of dedicated time of agility training are recommended, with one of those hours being with a weekly class. The more you can train at home between sessions, the better your dog will perform in this sport.

Outdoor Games – Frisbee, Fetch, And Other Fun

Schnoodles are fairly sturdy dogs that love running and playing outside, so prepare for your companion to be outside romping in nice weather whenever possible! Things like frisbee and fetch are the kinds of games that will tire your pup while using little of your own energy. You will need to get discs and balls that are easy on your dog's teeth.

Indoor Activities

During rainy and colder weather, you will need to find the right activities to play inside which will also tire out your canine:

The following are some alternatives to help expend your Schnoodle's energy:

- If you don't want to use a toy for chase, try getting your Schnoodle to chase a laser pointer. This may or may not work as your Schnoodle may realize that he can't catch it. If he doesn't seem to mind though, it is a terrific way to get rid of that energy on rainy or chilly days!

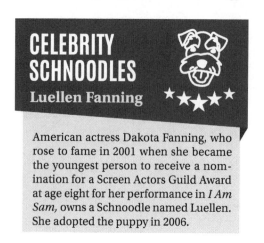

CELEBRITY SCHNOODLES
Luellen Fanning ★★★★★

American actress Dakota Fanning, who rose to fame in 2001 when she became the youngest person to receive a nomination for a Screen Actors Guild Award at age eight for her performance in *I Am Sam*, owns a Schnoodle named Luellen. She adopted the puppy in 2006.

- Puzzle toys are a fun way to get your dog to move around without you having to do much. Most puzzle toys are food based, so the dog will need to figure out how to get the treats out. If you use these, do keep that in mind since your dog isn't likely to work off the extra calories consumed from puzzle treats.

- You can create obstacle courses in or around your home, which would be

*Photo Courtesy
of Jennifer Henry-Smith*

Photo Courtesy
of Sue Mitgang

especially great for Giant Schnoodles. Just be careful not to make the course too difficult for your dog. You want him to have fun without getting hurt.

- Find some advanced training exercises, such as dancing, rollover, and playing dead. This can be time consuming, but your dog will love the extra attention and will have gotten plenty of mental stimulation.

Hide And Seek

Hide and seek is a game you can play once your dog understands proper behavior in the home. Since your Schnoodle will probably hear you wherever you hide, you can also make it a game of hide the toy. If you distract your pup while someone else hides the toy, your Schnoodle will have a fun time trying to locate it!

Training As A Therapy Dog

If your Schnoodle loves people and can remain calm enough, you might train him to work as a therapy dog. Performing this work on a regular basis might not be your final goal, but your dog can certainly visit people in nursing homes and other locations from time to time.

Becoming a therapy dog requires a lot of training, and not all Schnoodles are cut-out for this type of work; neither are all owners the perfect therapy dog trainer. However, if you both have the right temperament and dedication, this is an avenue that can keep your dog active and mentally engaged while making people smile. Check out the American Kennel Club's detailed article, "How to Train a Therapy Dog", to find out what is involved in turning your Schnoodle into a working pup.

CHAPTER 14
Grooming – Productive Bonding

"As the owner of four grooming shops, I can say that Schnoodles defi-nitely need their ears plucked every time they go to the groomers. This will help to prevent ear infections. As for how often they should come in. it depends on their coat. Some need to come in every 4 to 6 weeks and others 8 to 10 weeks."

ANGELA DENNY
Angela's Schnoodles

The effort needed for grooming your Schnoodle will depend on which parent your dog takes after. This is particularly true when considering the quality of his coat. Both breeds have similar aspects in terms of grooming needs, but they also have their own individual weaknesses. If your Schnoodle takes after his Schnauzer parent, his coat will be easier to groom but will still take some time.

In addition, there are the other grooming tasks you will need to do, including taking care of your Schnoodle's teeth and toenails.

Grooming Tools

You don't need a lot of tools to properly groom your Schnoodle. However, make sure you have the following on hand:
- A slicker or pin brush. (Bark Space provides some details on the different types of brushes.)
- Grooming comb. (This one is optional but can help curlier fur look fluffier.)
- Detangling spray is an excellent product that prevents tangling of your dog's coat, especially if it is more Poodle-like.
- Shampoo (Check Bark Space for the latest recommendations.)
- Nail trimmers
- Toothbrush and toothpaste. (Check the American Kennel Club for the latest recommendations.)

Photo Courtesy
of Dara Davis

Coat Management

Several factors may necessitate skipping the groomer and giving your dog a haircut at home. Grooming your dog can be a daunting endeavor, and it may take a few tries to get the haircut just the way you like it. David Colman, a writer for the *New York Times* and a proud dog owner, often cuts his Schnauzer's hair. Colman recommends investing in quality clippers and finding a dedicated space that's easy and practical to clean up. Make sure to do your research before reaching for the clippers—and take your time!

Designer breeds are notoriously difficult to predict when it comes to managing their coats. This is especially true with Schnoodles and with Doodle mixes because these breeds have coats similar to a Poodle.

At the least, you will need to brush your adult Schnoodle twice a week. If your dog's coat is more like a Poodle's fur, plan to brush your dog three or four times a week. Beyond that, if you want to have the fur styled like the Poodle parent's coat, you can. If you prefer a more mellow approach, as long as you maintain the brushing routine, that is fine, too. Since Schnoodles are considered hypoallergenic dogs, you aren't going to spend too much time cleaning up fur around the house after grooming.

Puppies

The difficulty when grooming a puppy is fairly universal because puppies are notorious for squirming! Nonetheless, a daily brushing can not only reduce how much your puppy sheds, but it helps build a bond with your dog. Yes, it will be a bit challenging in the beginning because puppies don't sit still for prolonged periods of time; there will be a lot of wiggling and attempts to play. Trying to tell your puppy that the brush is not a toy clearly won't work so be patient during each brushing session!

On the other hand, your pup will be so adorable, you probably won't mind a grooming session taking a bit longer than expected. Just make sure you let your pup know grooming is serious business and playing comes after grooming. Otherwise, your Schnoodle is going to always try to play, which will make brushing him more time-consuming.

Try planning to brush your puppy after a vigorous exercise session so your Schnoodle has far less energy. You can plan to brush once a week to establish a good bond with your puppy. If you find your puppy has trouble sitting still, you can make brushing sessions shorter but more than once a day until he gets used to the routine.

Photo Courtesy
of Derek & Laura Lieberman

Adult Dogs

Brushing your dog at least twice a week is adequate to get rid of his dead skin cells and loose fur. Depending on your Schnoodle's size and type of coat, this could be a time-consuming effort – the larger the dog, the more time it takes to fully groom him. Grooming mitts can make this task faster because it allows you to brush a large section of the coat with each stroke. Always look for skin problems, lumps, flea or tick bites, and other problems when you brush your buddy. This will indicate a potential problem, which you should keep an eye on with a trip to the vet if symptoms are severe.

If you rescued an adult Schnoodle, it may take a little while to get the dog used to being brushed frequently. If your dog does not feel comfortable in the beginning when you brush his fur, you can work the routine into your schedule, just like his training, so he will get accustomed to the task.

Senior Dogs

You can brush your senior dog more often if you would like, as the extra affection and time you give him will likely be welcome. After all, he's slowing down, and just relaxing with you will be enjoyable for him, (and the warmth of your hands will feel really good on his aging body). Grooming sessions are an appropriate time to check for problems while giving your older pup a nice massage to ease any pain. Look for any changes to the skin, such as bumps or fatty lumps. These may need to be mentioned to the vet during a regular visit if the bumps or lumps are large.

Three Primary Styles

While your dog's coat is not predictable, most Schnoodles do have coats that can be easily styled. There is a wide range of looks for each and every Schnoodle. A quick search online shows you just how versatile that coat can be. Nonetheless, there are three popular looks that most people embrace:

- The Puppy Cut is considered low maintenance since it cuts the fur close to the skin; it is usually one to two inches long right after the trim. If you choose this cut for your dog, brushing it is a lot easier (though you should stick to several times a week). This also means a lot more visits to the groomer to keep the fur short.

- The Teddy Bear Cut sounds as adorable as it looks! Usually this is used on smaller Schnoodles. Grooming is about as easy as the Puppy Cut since most of the body fur is cut short, but the fur around the head is a rounder style. If your Schnoodle has the signature Schnauzer mustache, this look highlights that mustache and is particularly sweet. It also means you are going to need to do more grooming around the face.

127

- The Shaggy Look is accomplished by allowing the fur to grow as it wishes – no cutting. You will need to keep up with the regular grooming and may need to spend more time working out matted fur and dirt (depending on your dog's fur...curly vs. wavy). You will also need to brush your dog more often to make sure dirt isn't trapped in his longer fur.

Each of these styles has its own benefits - beyond looks. If you don't mind more frequent visits to the groomer and less time with regular brushing sessions, a shorter look is better for you. If you would rather have the scheduled brushing sessions and fewer trips to the groomer, then a shaggier look is for you.

Allergies

Some Schnoodles have skin allergies. If your Schnoodle is suffering from hot spots, or if you notice his coat is thinning, then you should look for the following allergic reactions:

- Wounds take longer to heal
- Weak immune system
- Aching joints
- Hair is falling out
- Ear infections

Regular brushing makes you aware of the health of your Schnoodle's coat. This will help you identify when your little dear is suffering from allergies so you can take him to the vet immediately.

Bath Time

Your Schnoodle will need a bath about once a month unless he gets really dirty. Avoid washing him too often since it can irritate your dog's skin and remove necessary oils in his fur.

Whenever you go exploring or hiking with your Schnoodle, most likely you will need to bathe your canine after each adventure. Make sure the water isn't too cold or too hot but comfortably warm, and you should always avoid getting his head wet. Washing your dog's face is covered in the next section.

1. Gather everything you will need before you start your dog's bath. At a minimum, you need the following:

    a. Shampoo and conditioners made specifically for dogs

    b. Cup for pouring water (if bathing in a tub)

    c. Towels

    d. Brushes for after the drying process

    e. Non-slip tub mat if you use a tub

2. If you bathe your dog outside, you will also need buckets and a hose to rinse him off.

3. Take your Schnoodle out for a walk. This will tire your dog and make him a little hotter, which will make your dog less fearful – he might even appreciate the bath's cooling effect.

4. Run the water, making sure the temperature is lukewarm but not hot, especially if you have just finished a walk. If you are washing your Schnoodle in a bathtub, you only need enough water to cover your pup's stomach. Do not fully cover your dog's body.

5. Pick up your dog, if you are using a bathtub, and talk in a strong, confident voice.

6. Place the dog in the tub and use the cup to wash the dog. Don't use too much soap – it isn't necessary. You can fully soak the dog starting at the neck and going to the rump. It is fine to get him wet and to suds him up all at once, or you can do it a little at a time if your dog is very wiggly. Just make sure you don't get any water on his head.

Photo Courtesy of Lisa Schmidt

7. Talk to your dog while you are bathing him keeping in mind you need to talk with confidence.

8. Make sure you don't pour water on your dog's head or in his eyes or ears. Use a wet hand and gently scrub. (Follow the steps in the next section to properly – and carefully – wash your dog's face and ears.)

9. When you rinse, make sure to brush up against the fur so there is no shampoo left.

10. Take your Schnoodle out of the water and towel him dry.

11. Brush your dog when you are finished.

12. Give him a treat if he was particularly upset about the bath.

You can use these practices with other kinds of bathing, such as outside or at a public washing facility; modify them, as necessary.

The first few times you bathe your dog, pay attention to the things that bother or scare him. If he is afraid of running water, make sure you don't have the water running when your dog is in the tub. If he moves around a lot when you start to apply the shampoo, it could indicate the smell is too strong. You need to modify the process to make it as comfortable for your dog as possible.

Keep a calm, loving tone as you wash your dog to make the process a little easier next time. Sure, your Schnoodle may whine, throw a tantrum, or wiggle excessively, but a calm reaction will teach your dog that bathing is a necessary part of being a member of the pack.

If these steps are not quite right for your dog's coat, there are many websites that suggest different ways of grooming your Schnoodle:

- How to Groom a Schnoodle Dog (https://www.cuteness.com/article/ groom-schnoodle-dog)
- How to Groom a Schnoodle Dog (https://www.wikihow.pet/ Groom-a-Schnoodle-Dog)

Cleaning Eyes And Ears

When bathing your dog, use a washcloth to wash his face and ears, and ALWAYS avoid getting water in his ears, which can lead to problems.

Since both parent breeds tend to have a lot of fur around their eyes and ears, you will need to make weekly checks in those areas. Regularly checking your dog's ears (once a week) can help you detect infections early. Look for the following behaviors for signs of a problem:

- Frequent head shaking or tilting
- Regular scratching at ears
- Swollen or red ears
- A smell or discharge from the ears

If you notice any problems with your Schnoodle's ears, make an appointment with your vet. Never try to treat an infection on your own; hydrogen peroxide, cotton swabs, and other cleaning tools should never be used in a dog's ears. Your vet can show you how to clean your dog's ears correctly if infections become common.

Schnoodles have a few genetic eye and ear conditions (See Chapter 16) so take time to always check your dog's eyes while you are grooming him.

The biggest threat to your dog's eyes is probably going to be the dirt that can stick to the fur around this area. This is one reason why many people keep this fur shorter – especially if your Schnoodle has the large Schnauzer eyebrows.

Cataracts are a fairly common problem for all dogs as they age. If you see cloudy eyes, have your Schnoodle checked. If he's developing cataracts, you may need to have them removed because cataracts can lead to blindness.

Trimming Nails

Cutting a Schnoodle's nails can be difficult because dogs can be sensitive about touching their paws. Odds are they will have dark nails, which makes it difficult to cut the correct length without accidently cutting the quick. It's best to have an expert cut your dog's nails until you understand how trimming is done. If you have never cut a dog's nails, ask a professional, like a groomer or a vet, to teach you the steps involved because nails can bleed a lot if cut properly. If you know how to trim a dog's nails, make sure to have some styptic powder nearby in case you cut the nail too close.

If you want to trim your dog's nails yourself, there are nail grinders that can help lessen your worry about cutting them to the quick, but you will need to make sure you don't grind too much off the nail. Seek help from a professional before using the grinder, keep your dog calm during the process, and always think of your dog's safety first.

To know when your pup needs his nails cut, listen for clicking sounds on the hard surfaces when your dog is walking. Those clicking sounds indicate you should trim your dog's nails on a more frequent basis. As a general rule, once a month is recommended.

Oral Health And Brushing Your Dog's Teeth

It is recommended that you brush your Schnoodle's teeth at least twice a week, but it is best to make it a daily task in order to reduce tartar buildup. Since a Schnoodle will likely be up in your face often, daily brushing also helps to reduce bad breath! You probably will want to learn to do the brushing yourself instead of visiting the vet. It's a good idea to learn this skill - especially when his breath smells bad or he eats something with a foul odor. These situations mean a couple of brushings a day might be needed in order to keep your dog's breath smelling clean and fresh.

Again, you have to learn to be patient and keep teeth cleaning from being an all-out fight with your dog. Brushing a dog's teeth is a little weird, and your Schnoodle may not be terribly happy with someone putting stuff in his mouth. However, once he is accustomed to it, the task will likely only take a few minutes a day.

Always use a toothpaste that is made for dogs; human toothpaste can be toxic for them. There are assorted flavors of dog toothpaste, which will make it easier when brushing his teeth, and it could also be entertaining as he tries to eat the meat-flavored toothpaste!

The following are the steps for brushing your pup's teeth:

1. Put a little toothpaste on your finger and hold it out to your dog.

2. Let your dog lick the toothpaste from your finger.

3. Praise your dog for trying something new.

4. Put a little toothpaste on your finger, lift your dog's upper lip, and begin to rub in circles along your Schnoodle's gums. Your pup will likely make it difficult by constantly trying to lick your finger. Give your puppy praise when he doesn't lick the toothpaste or doesn't wiggle too much.

   a. Try to move your finger in a circular motion. This will be very tricky, especially with those sharp baby teeth.

   b. Try to keep the puppy still without putting the little pooch in a vise. As your puppy gets bigger, he'll need to know how to voluntarily sit for the cleaning process.

5. Try to massage both the top and bottom gums. It is likely the first few times you won't be able to do much more than get your finger in your dog's mouth and that's okay. Over time, your puppy will learn to listen because general behavioral training will reinforce listening to your commands.

6. Stay positive. No, you probably won't be able to clean the puppy's teeth properly for a while, and that is perfectly fine - as long as you keep working at it patiently and consistently.

Once your dog seems comfortable with having his teeth brushed with your finger, try the same steps with a canine toothbrush. (It could take a couple of weeks before you can graduate to a toothbrush.)

CHAPTER 15
General Health Issues: Allergies, Parasites, and Vaccinations

Environmental factors largely determine whether or not your dog gets parasites. For example, if you live near woods, your dog is at a greater risk of ticks than a dog that lives in the city. Your dog may also have allergic reactions to the environment around your home or in a location where you go exploring together. Talk to your vet about all potential environmental risks.

The Role Of Your Veterinarian

Scheduled veterinary visits, routine vaccinations, and regular checkups make for a healthy Schnoodle. If your dog seems sluggish or less excited than usual, it could be a sign there is something wrong with him. Fortunately, the breed's personality tends to make it easy to tell when a dog isn't feeling well. Annual visits to the vet will eliminate any problems that might be slowly draining the energy or the health from your dog.

Regular checkups also make sure that your Schnoodle is aging well. If your dog shows symptoms of a potential problem, an early diagnosis will address the problem. You and your vet will create a plan to manage any pain or problems that come with your dog's aging process. He may recommend adjustments to your schedule to accommodate his aging body and his diminishing abilities. This will ensure that you can keep having fun together without hurting your dog.

Vets can provide treatment or preventive medication for parasites and other microscopic threats, which your dog

CELEBRITY SCHNOODLES

Willie the Schnoodle

★★★★★

Willie the Schnoodle has lived a rags-to-riches story. Abandoned as a puppy in New Orleans, Willie was adopted by a globe-trotting web consultant named Justin Bhagat from Canada. The duo has traveled the world, from Italy to New York to Sweden, and everywhere in between. Willie and Justin have seen it all. Together, the duo visited twelve countries in just five years!

might encounter on a daily basis. These attacks can happen when he is playing outside or when he is exposed to dogs or other animals.

Allergies

The scientific name for environmental allergies is atopic dermatitis. However, it is difficult to know if the problem is environmental or if it is food you are feeding your dog.

The following symptoms can be seen when either type of allergy is present:

- Itching/scratching, particularly around the face
- Hot spots
- Ear infections
- Skin infections
- Runny eyes and nose (not as common)

Dogs often develop allergies when they are between one and five years old. Once they develop an allergy, canines never outgrow the problem. Dog allergies are usually a result of allergens (such as dust, mold, or pollen), which irritate the skin or nasal passage.

Since the symptoms are the same for food and environmental allergies, your vet will help determine the cause. If your dog has a food allergy, all you have to do is change the food that you give him. If he has an environmental allergy, he will need medication, just as humans do. If environmental, you will need to determine if the problem is seasonal or year-round, so you know when to treat your dog.

As with humans, completely eliminating the problem isn't possible; there is only so much you can do to change the environment around your dog. There are several types of medications that can help your dog become less sensitive to the allergens:

- **Antibacterial/Antifungal** – These treatments only address the problems that come with allergies; shampoos, pills, and creams usually do not directly treat the allergy itself.

- **Anti-inflammatories** – These are over-the-counter medications, which are comparable to allergy medicine for people. Don't give your dog any medication without first consulting with the vet. You will need to monitor your dog to see if he has any adverse effects. If your dog is lethargic, has diarrhea, or shows signs of dehydration, consult with your vet immediately.

- **Immunotherapy** – This method is a series of shots which can help reduce your dog's sensitivity to whatever he is allergic to. This is something you can do at home after learning how to give the shots from your vet. Scientists are also developing an oral version of this medication to make it easier to take care of your dog.

- **Topical** – This medication tends to be a type of shampoo and conditioner that will remove any allergens from your dog's fur. Giving your dog a warm (not hot) bath can also help relieve itching.

To determine the best treatment for your situation, talk with your vet regarding available medications.

Inhalant And Environmental Allergies

Inhalant allergies are caused by things like dust, pollen, mold, and even dog dander. Your dog might scratch at a particular hot spot, or he might paw at his eyes and ears. Some dogs have runny noses and sneeze prolifically, in addition to scratching.

Contact Allergies

Contact allergies mean that your dog has touched something that triggers an allergic reaction. Things like wool, chemicals in a flea treatment, and certain grasses can trigger irritation in a dog's skin, even causing discoloration. If left untreated, the allergic reaction can cause the affected area to emit a strong odor or cause fur loss.

Like food allergies, contact allergies are easy to treat because once you know what is irritating your dog's skin, you can remove the problem.

Fleas And Ticks

Make it a habit to check for ticks after every outing into the woods or near long grass or wild plants. Comb through your dog's fur and check his skin for signs of irritation and for any parasites. Since you will be doing this several times a week, you should be able to recognize when there's a change, such as a new bump.

Fleas are problematic because they're far more mobile than ticks. The best way to look for fleas is to make it a regular part of your brushing sessions. If you see black specks on the flea comb after brushing through your dog's fur, this could be a sign of fleas.

Instead of using a comb, you can also put your dog on a white towel and run your hand over the fur. Fleas and flea dirt are likely to fall onto the towel. Fleas often are seen on the stomach, so you may notice them when your pup wants a belly rub. You can also look for behavioral indicators, such as incessant scratching and licking. If fleas are a problem, you will need to use flea preventative products on a regular basis once your puppy has reached the appropriate age.

Along with being annoying, both fleas and ticks can carry parasites and illnesses that can be passed on to you and your family. Ticks notoriously carry Lyme disease, which can be debilitating or deadly if untreated. Lyme disease symptoms include headaches, fever, and fatigue. The bite itself often has a red circle around it that may grow. Once attached to your dog's skin, he will likely start to act sluggish. Watch for a circular rash to appear, and whether you see one or not, go to the vet to have your dog checked out.

If the tick hasn't latched on, you can just remove it – it hasn't yet bitten your dog. Ticks will fall off your dog once they are full, so if you find a tick on your dog, it will either be looking for a place to latch onto your dog or it will be feeding. Use the following steps to remove the tick if it has latched onto your dog:

*Photo Courtesy
of Renae Facundus*

1. Apply rubbing alcohol to the area where the tick is located.
2. Use tweezers to pull the tick off your dog. Do not use your fingers because infections are transmitted through blood, and you don't want the tick to latch onto you.
3. Place the tick in a bag and make sure it is secure so that it does not fall out.
4. Examine the spot where the tick was to make sure it is fully removed. Sometimes the head will remain under the dog's skin, so you will need to make sure all of the tick has been removed.
5. Set up a meeting with the vet to have your dog checked. Make sure to bring the bagged tick with you.

The FDA has issued a warning about some store-bought treatments for fleas and ticks. Treatments can be applied monthly, or you can purchase a collar for constant protection. Either way, make sure the treatment does not contain isoxazoline, which can have a negative effect on some pets. (This chemical is found in Bravecto, Nexgard, Credelio, and Simparica.)

Most ingredients in these treatments are safe if the proper dose is used. If you use a product that is meant for a larger dog, the effects can be toxic to your smaller dog. Consult your vet for recommended treatments and issue the appropriate dose of flea and tick repellant for your dog's size and his needs. When you start applying the treatment, watch your dog for the following issues:

- Diarrhea/vomiting
- Lethargy
- Trembling
- Seizures

Take your dog to the vet if you notice any of these issues.

Never use any cat product designed for a dog and vice versa. If your dog is sick, pregnant, or nursing, you may need to look for an alternative treatment. Flea collars are generally not recommended in this situation because they are known to cause problems in pets and people. If you have a cat or young children, you should choose one of the other options for keeping fleas and ticks away. This is because flea collars contain an ingredient that is lethal to felines and which might be carcinogenic to humans.

Packaging on flea treatments will advise you when to begin treating your dog based on his current age and size. Different brands have different recommendations, and you don't want to start treating your puppy too early. There are also important steps to applying the treatment. Make sure you understand all of the steps before purchasing the flea treatment.

If you want to use natural products instead of chemicals, research the alternatives and decide what works best for your Schnoodle. Verify that any natural products work before you buy them and make sure you consult with your vet. Establish a regular monthly schedule and add it to your calendar so you remember to consistently treat your dog for fleas and ticks.

Parasitic Worms

Although worms are a less common problem than fleas and ticks, they can be far more dangerous. The following lists the types of worms that you should be aware of:

- Heartworms
- Roundworms
- Whipworms
- Hookworms
- Tapeworms

Unfortunately, there isn't an easy-to-recognize set of symptoms to help identify when your dog has worms. However, you can keep an eye out for the following symptoms, and if your dog shows any of these warning signs, schedule a visit to the vet:

- Your Schnoodle is unexpectedly lethargic for at least a few days.
- Patches of fur begin to fall out (This will be noticeable if you brush your Schnoodle regularly.) or if you notice patchy spaces in your dog's coat.
- Your dog's stomach becomes distended (expands) and looks like a potbelly.
- Your Schnoodle begins coughing, vomiting, has diarrhea, or has a loss in appetite.

If you aren't sure about any symptom, it's always best to get to the vet as soon as possible.

Heartworms

Heartworms are a significant threat to your dog's health and can be deadly as they can both slow and stop blood flow. As such, you should consistently treat your dog with heartworm protection.

Fortunately, there are medications that prevent your dog from developing heartworms. To prevent this deadly problem, you can give your dog a chewable medication, topical medicine, or you can request shots.

The heartworm parasite is carried by mosquitoes, which are nearly impossible to avoid in most regions of the country, and it is a condition which is costly and time-consuming to treat...more importantly to cure. Alleviating the disease is well worth the work in order to keep your pup healthy and happy.

The following are the steps involved in treating your dog for heartworms:

- The vet will draw blood for testing, which can cost as much as $1,000.
- Treatment will begin with some initial medications, including antibiotics and anti-inflammatory drugs.
- Following a month of the initial medication, your vet will give your dog three shots over the course of two months.

From the time of diagnosis until the confirmation your dog is free of heartworms, you will need to treat your dog very carefully. Caution is needed when you exercise your dog because the worms are in your dog's heart and that inhibits blood flow. This means raising your dog's heartbeat too much could kill him. Your vet will tell you how best to exercise your canine during this time. Considering your Schnoodle is likely to be energetic, this is going to be a very rough time for both you and your dog.

Treatment will continue after the shots are complete. After approximately six months, your vet will conduct another blood test to ensure the worms are gone.

Once your dog is cleared of the parasites, you will need to begin medicating your dog against heartworms in the future. There will also be lasting damage to your dog's heart, so you will need to ensure that your dog does not over-exercise.

Intestinal Worms: Hookworms, Roundworms, Tapeworms, And Whipworms

All four of these worms thrive in your dog's intestinal tract, and they get there when your dog eats something contaminated with them. The following are the most common ways dogs ingest worms:

- Feces
- Small hosts, such as fleas, cockroaches, earthworks, and rodents
- Soil, including licking it from their fur and paws
- Contaminated water
- Mother's milk (If the mother has worms, she can pass it to young puppies when they nurse.)

The following are the most common symptoms and problems caused by intestinal parasites:

- Anemia
- Blood loss
- Coughing
- Dehydration
- Diarrhea
- Large intestine inflammation
- Weight loss
- A pot-bellied appearance

If a dog lies in soil with hookworm larvae, the parasite can burrow through the canine's skin. Vets will conduct a diagnostic test to determine if your dog has this parasite, and if your dog does have hookworms, they will prescribe a de-wormer. You should visit a doctor yourself because humans can get hookworms, too.

Roundworms are quite common, and at some point in their lives, most dogs have to be treated for them. They primarily eat the digested food in your dog's stomach, getting the nutrients your dog needs. It is possible for larvae to remain in your dog's stomach even after all of the adult worms have been eradicated, and mother dogs can pass these larvae to their puppies. If your Schnoodle is pregnant, her puppies should be checked periodically to make sure the inactive larvae are not passed on to the puppies. The mother

Photo Courtesy
of Cindy Hood

will also need to go through the same testing to make sure the worms don't make her sick.

Tapeworms are usually eaten when they are eggs and are usually carried by fleas or from the feces of other animals who also have tapeworms. The eggs develop in the canine's small intestine until they reach the adult stage. Over time, parts of the tapeworm will break off and can be seen in your dog's waste. If this happens, you should be very thorough when cleaning up any waste so other animals will not contract tapeworms, also. While tapeworms are not usually fatal, they can cause weight loss and give your dog a potbelly. (The size of your dog's stomach depends on how big the worms grow in your dog's intestines.)

Your vet can test your dog for tapeworms and can prescribe medication to take care of the problem. The medication might include chewable tablets, regular tablets, or a powder that can be sprinkled on your dog's food. There is a minimal risk of humans catching tapeworms, but children are the greatest risk because they play in areas frequented by dogs. Be sure children wash their hands carefully if playing in areas used by your dog. It is also possible to contract tapeworms if a person swallows a flea, which is feasible if your dog and home have a serious infestation.

Whipworms grow in the large intestine, and when in large numbers, they can be fatal. Their name is indicative of the appearance with their tails, which are thinner than their upper section. Like the other worms, you will need to have your dog tested to determine if he has acquired whipworms.

Staying current with flea treatments, disposing of your pet's waste, and making sure your Schnoodle does not eat trash or animal waste will help prevent your dog from getting these parasites.

If your dog has hookworms or roundworms, these can be spread to you from your dog through skin contact. Being treated at the same time as your Schnoodle will help stop the vicious cycle of continually trading off which of you has worms.

Medication to prevent these four parasites can often be included in your dog's heartworm medication. Be sure to speak with your vet regarding the different options.

Vaccinating Your Schnoodle

Vaccination schedules are routine for most dog breeds, including Schnoodles. Make sure to add this information to your calendar, and until your puppy has completed his vaccinations, he should avoid contact with other dogs.

The following list can help you schedule your Schnoodle's vaccinations:

Timeline	Shot		
6 to 8 weeks	Bordetella Lyme	Leptospira Influenza Virus-H3N8	DHPP – First shot Influenza Virus-H3N2
10 to 12 weeks	Leptospira Lyme	DHPP – Second Rabies shot Influenza Virus-H3N8	Influenza Virus-H3N2
14 to 16 weeks	DHPP – Third shot		
Annually	Leptospira Lyme	Bordetella Influenza Virus-H3N8	Rabies Influenza Virus-H3N2
Every 3 Years	DHPP Booster	Rabies (if opted for longer duration vaccination)	

These shots protect your dog against a range of ailments. Keep in mind these shots should be a part of your dog's annual vet visit so you can continue to keep your pup safe!

Holistic Alternatives

Wanting to prevent exposure to chemical treatments for your dog makes sense, and there are many good reasons why people are moving to more holistic methods. However, if you decide to go with holistic medication, talk with your vet first about reputable options. You can also seek out Schnoodle experts for recommendations before you start trying any holistic methods of care.

It is possible something like massage therapy can help your dog, especially as he ages. Massages help with the aching bones and joints, just like with a person. Before using massage therapy with your dog, consider the potential problems your breed is prone to experiencing, which could prevent problems due to the treatment. Even chiropractic therapy is available for dogs, but you will need to be sure to find a reputable chiropractor for your pup, so the treatment doesn't do more harm than good. Follow recommendations on reputable, holistic Schnoodle websites to provide the best, safest care for your dog.

CHAPTER 16
Genetic Health Concerns Common to the Schnoodle

As with all designer breeds, it is impossible to know exactly what health issues your canine will experience. Trying to guess what ailments a dog is likely to inherit is tricky at best. Therefore, the best way to keep your canine healthy is to be aware of the ailments that are common to both of the original breeds. (Details regarding genetic and common ailments of Schnoodles can be found in Chapter 3.)

Making sure the parents are healthy increases the likelihood that your puppy will remain healthy, too. However, there is still a chance your dog will have one of these documented problems even if the parents do not, so you will still need to keep an eye on your friend.

Photo Courtesy of Jordan Drake

Common Schnauzer Health Issues

Since Schnauzers come in three different sizes, there are different sets of health problems for the different stages of your dog's life. However, most of the conditions are fairly universal across all sizes because they originated with the Standard Schnauzer.

Cushing's Disease

Also known as hyperadrenocorticism, this disease occurs when a dog's adrenal glands produce excess amounts of the hormone cortisone. It is easy to mistake this disease due to your dog's aging. Symptoms of hyperadrenocorticism include excessive drinking, frequent bathroom use, loss of appetite and hair, and weight gain.

If you notice your dog gaining weight, drinking more, or having accidents around the home, take him to the vet. Cushing's Disease is treatable, so the earlier you catch it, the better your dog's quality of life. Treatment usually includes medication, though in the worst case, it may require surgery.

Hip And Elbow Dysplasia

Hip and elbow dysplasia are common ailments for medium and larger-size dogs. Their diet (Chapter 12) as a puppy can help minimize the problem when they become adults. Both types of dysplasia occur when a dog's hips and leg sockets become malformed, which often leads to arthritis. The condition can be detected by the time a dog becomes an adult (around two years old for a Schnoodle). The only way to detect dysplasia is through X-rays.

This is a problem that your Schnoodle may try to hide because he won't want to slow down. Your adult dog will walk a little more stiffly or may pant even when it's not hot weather. The condition usually becomes more obvious as a dog nears his golden years. Similar to the way older people tend to change their gait to accommodate pain, your dog may do the same. Getting up may be a little more difficult in the beginning and will likely get worse as he ages.

While surgery is an option in severe cases, most dogs can benefit from less invasive treatments:

- Anti-inflammatory medications – These medications may be all your dog needs; however, dogs should never take large doses of anti-inflammatory drugs because they can damage your dog's kidneys. Always talk with your vet before administering these medications.

- Lower the amount of high-impact exercise your dog experiences - especially on wooden floors, tile, concrete, or other hard surfaces.

Most Schnoodles love to swim, so you can follow a swimming regimen instead. This change will keep him active without the jarring motions of walking on hard surfaces.

- Joint fluid-modifiers
- Physical therapy
- Weight loss (for dogs who are overweight or obese)

Dental Issues

Schnauzers are notorious for their dental issues. Breeding has made all sizes of this breed more susceptible to gum disease. To ensure a healthy mouth, you should brush your dog's teeth on a regular basis. If your dog takes after the Schnauzer's poor dental health, then daily brushing is recommended! This may occasionally include taking him to a professional for a more thorough cleaning.

Eye Problems

Schnauzers usually develop several different eye issues, but the problems tend to be as much a product of age as of genetics. Still, you should know about the potential issues to make sure you take proper care of your pup's adorable eyes.

Cataracts

Cataracts are a fairly common problem for all dogs as they age. If your dog's eyes appear to be cloudy, take him to the vet. If he's developing cataracts, your vet may have to remove them - cataracts can lead to blindness.

Entropion

Entropion is when the dog's eyelids roll inward, damaging the cornea as the eyelashes scratch it. The corrective surgery that fixes this problem can cause another eye disorder, ectropion. This is when the lower eyelid droops down so that you can see the soft pink tissue under the eye. While ectropion is not a serious problem, it does increase the likelihood of eye infections.

Progressive Retinal Atrophy (Pra)

Roughly 10% of Schnoodles have PRA, which causes a sensitivity to light because of problems with the retina. Puppies should be tested, so if you adopt your puppy from a breeder, you should obtain a guarantee against this particular problem.

Dogs with this condition usually start presenting with night blindness, which can make your dog more nervous. If you look at your dog's eyes, they may also reflect light more as the eyes deteriorate. The ailment affects both eyes, so the problem would show in both places.

There is no treatment for PRA. You will need to learn to accommodate your dog's failing sight over time.

Heart Problems

Schnauzers of all sizes have some genetic heart issues; different size dogs are prone to different conditions.

Miniature Schnauzers can have heart murmurs or abnormal rhythms. Neither of these tend to be too serious, but your vet should check for these issues during each visit since they could be symptoms of a more severe problem. Heart disease is the most common cause of death in Miniature Schnauzers, with deformation of the heart valves being the usual reason. Murmurs and abnormal rhythms could be an early warning sign that there is a deeper problem.

SCHNOODLES AT WORK
Anything's Paw-sible

Anything's Paw-sible is a therapy dog nonprofit in Texas run by Kristin Cashon, and geared towards supporting local students. Cashon started the organization because her daughter benefited from a therapy dog after being diagnosed with OCD. In August 2020, the organization added a new therapy dog, a Schnoodle named Jack, to help students at Hook Elementary in Stephenville, Texas. Jack will help students with testing and reading anxiety, as well as the uncertainty of returning to school during the coronavirus pandemic.

Standard Schnauzers often have a condition called pulmonic stenosis, which results in partial obstruction of blood flow. This causes the heart to work extremely hard to pump blood to the lungs and wears down the heart rather quickly. If your dog coughs, seems to have trouble breathing, or appears sluggish without any obvious reason, take him to the vet so he can be checked. Unfortunately, this condition may require surgery to correct the problem.

Bloat/Gastric Dilatation Volvulus (Gdv)

Standard Schnauzers and Giant Schnauzers may acquire GDV, which is more commonly known as bloat. It is a problem with dog breeds that have larger chests. Their stomach can fill with gases, causing the stomach to bloat. In the worst cases, the gas can cause the stomach to twist, cutting off the entrance and exit to the stomach. Nothing can enter or leave your dog's stomach once the stomach twists like this. While the bloat stage is not lethal, once the stomach twists, it can kill your dog.

This is not a genetic disease, but a physiological problem because of the structure of large dogs with deep chests and a smaller mid-section. This combination is what makes their stomach prone to bloat and twisting.

Prevention is the best way of dealing with this problem. While your dog can undergo surgery to keep the stomach from twisting, this may not be the best method of treatment for Schnoodles (see MDS).

You can reduce the risk of this problem by taking the following measures:

- Feed your dog two or three times a day (not just one meal).
- Add wet dog food to kibble (if you feed your dog commercial dog food).
- Ensure the dry dog food is calcium rich.

Hypothyroidism

This is a problem that is also found in humans (and many other dog breeds). Hypothyroidism is a result of the dog (or person) not making enough thyroid hormone. This usually appears between the ages of two and six years and is noted by weight gain, lack of energy, and skin problems - such as dry or itchy skin.

A blood test is done to find out if a Schnoodle has hypothyroidism. Some vets will conduct the test annually as a preventative measure. If your dog has hypothyroidism, your vet will likely prescribe an oral medication.

Kidney Stones

One of the most common ailments in all sizes of Schnauzers is kidney stones. In fact, Miniature Schnauzers seem to have the problem more often than other sizes. Kidney stones are the same in dogs as in humans - small, crystallized particles form stones in the kidney and cause sharp pain. Whimpering with no obvious sign of a problem is often the first sign something is wrong. Other potential symptoms are an enlarged stomach, vomiting, sluggishness, difficulty going to the bathroom, and loss of appetite. If your dog yelps when you touch his stomach, that can also be a sign that he has kidney stones.

Since the symptoms seem to happen quickly, it often results in a visit to the emergency room. (Kidney stones are incredibly painful!) The most common treatment includes antibiotics and a strict diet to keep new stones from forming. If the stones are large or too hard, surgery may be required.

Myotonia Congenita

This is a genetic issue in Miniature Schnauzers, and it affects the dog's skeletal muscles. A dog with this disorder will experience their muscles remaining tense after being active. It is a fairly rare disorder that often presents when a Miniature Schnauzer is young and learning to walk.

Breeders should not be selling puppies that exhibit this problem, and it will be clear that a puppy is suffering within the first few weeks of life. However, if you have a dog with this problem, consult your vet about testing and about ways to help your dog. While the disease can cause some problems, such as raspy breathing or problem swallowing, it does not appear to affect a dog's lifespan.

Pancreatitis And Diabetes

Another ailment found in Miniature Schnauzers is pancreatitis, which is the inflammation of the pancreas. The pancreas is responsible for the production of insulin and digestive enzymes. If a dog has pancreatitis, they will vomit and have diarrhea as well as being lethargic. It could also cause your dog to have a fever, increasing the odds he will become dehydrated. This is potentially a fatal disease. If your dog has any of these symptoms, get him to the vet immediately! If he has pancreatitis, he will be put in intensive care for immediate treatment. Only a vet can treat this potentially fatal illness.

Like people, Schnauzers are prone to Diabetes, which can be further exacerbated or caused by pancreatitis. This is why it is critical to ensure your dog is on a healthy diet and does not become obese.

Comedo Syndrome

Comedo Syndrome is another illness that surfaces in Miniature Schnauzers and causes skin lesions that look like small scabs on the Schnauzer's back. They are often small, look similar to black heads, and are caused by defects in the dog's hair follicles. This condition is painful, but special shampoos can help to reduce the problem. You can also ask your vet about oral antibiotics or antiseptic wipes if the lesions get infected. There is no cure, but it is not a significant problem requiring much more than a little additional care when managing your dog's coat.

Common Poodle Health Issues

Most Poodle sizes have similar health issues, so it doesn't matter if the parent is a Miniature or Standard Poodle. Many of these problems have minimal health risks and are treatable if identified and treated early.

Addison's Disease

Addison's Disease can be a major health problem if your dog's adrenal gland is not producing enough of two hormones - aldosterone and cortisol. Aldosterone regulates your dog's electrolytes and hydration. Cortisol helps your dog deal with stress. It can also destroy your dog's immune system, cause tumors to form, and increase the risk of cancer.

The following are symptoms of Addison's disease:

- Dehydration
- Depression
- Diarrhea
- Excessive thirst
- Lethargy
- Poor appetite
- Weakness
- Weight loss
- Vomiting

If you notice these symptoms, take your dog to the vet as soon as possible for a diagnosis. If your vet determines your dog has Addison's disease, oral medication is typically recommended, and it is possible your dog will need to be medicated for the rest of his life. Your vet will monitor your dog to decide if that is necessary. Once your dog starts feeling the effects of the medication, he should be able to resume normal meals and exercise

Epilepsy

One of the scariest problems that occurs in Poodles is epilepsy; however, the ailment is largely scarier for you and your dog than it is dangerous. While epilepsy can be severe in some dogs, most often it is something that will require additional cuddling without medication.

The following list gives the wide range of symptoms connected to Epilepsy:

- Confusion
- Difficulty breathing
- Drooling
- Stiff limbs
- Sudden unconsciousness
- Strange movements, such as walking in place or pacing
- Unresponsiveness

If you notice any of these symptoms, you need to take your dog to the vet. Your vet will help you determine appropriate treatment.

Bloat/Gastric Dilatation And Volvulus (Gdv)

Larger Poodles, as well as larger Schnauzers, are equally susceptible to bloat.

Progressive Retinal Atrophy (Pra)

The problems and symptoms are the same for Poodles and Schnauzers.

Sebaceous Adenitis

This is a skin disease that destroys the sebaceous glands, which produce lubricating secretions and can cause scales and hair loss. It is not life-threatening – it is a cosmetic problem. Your dog probably won't even notice the problem unless he has another kind of skin infection, too (which can be promoted by the disease).

It is a genetic disease, so your vet will need details regarding the parents' health. If that is not possible, your vet will run a few tests to determine if it is something to worry about.

If your pup has sebaceous adenitis, the vet will likely suggest a topical or oral therapy to help reduce the effects. This treatment might also include an antibiotic to treat any secondary infections.

Luxating Patella

Luxating patella, when the kneecap slips out of place, is more common in Toy Poodles than in Standard Poodles. Treatment depends on the severity of the ailment. You should talk to your vet as a brace may be adequate for some dogs while others may require surgery.

Legg-Calve-Perthes Disease

Legg-Calve-Perthes disease is a degenerative bone disease that affects your dog's femurs. It is thought to be caused by a disruption in blood flow, which then weakens the bones. This can result in fractures and scarring to the surrounding tissue. One of the biggest concerns is that it typically leads to arthritis.

If a dog has this problem, you will notice limping of the effected leg. Touching the leg can be very painful for your dog, so you should go to the vet if you suspect your dog has this condition.

The disease is typically associated with smaller dogs, so it is less likely to be a problem if one of the parents is a Standard Poodle. If a Toy Poodle is a parent, your dog will be at greater risk.

In this instance, your vet may recommend pain medication. You will be expected to keep your dog in a healthy weight range. Severe cases may require surgery.

Von Willebrand Disease

A major health problem for Miniature and Standard Poodles, Von Willebrand disease, affects blood platelets by reducing the amount of proteins in the body. While Poodles are not at an elevated risk for this illness, it is serious, and there are no obvious symptoms associated with it. If your dog receives a cut that bleeds too much for too long, this might indicate your dog has the disease, and a trip to the vet is necessary.

Like MDS, dogs with Von Willebrand disease cannot receive typical medications, such as anti-inflammatories and penicillin because these are blood-thinning medications and will only make matters worse. Your vet will consider these restrictions and will recommend the best treatment.

Hip And Elbow Dysplasia

The larger a dog is, the more likely they will have one or both of these problems. The symptoms, diagnosis, and treatment are the same, regardless of breed.

Hyperthyroid And Hypothyroid

This problem is equally common among both Poodles and Schnauzers.

Common Owner Mistakes

In addition to genetic problems, there are things you can do that could unintentionally damage your dog's health; these mistakes are related to diet and to exercise levels. In the puppy stage, it is a difficult balance to strike as your puppy is curious and enthusiastic. Even when he is a fully grown dog, you have to make sure you are minimizing how much stress is placed on your Schnoodle's body. Weight management is one important way of keeping your dog healthy. You need to balance your dog's diet with his level of activity to prevent exacerbation of hip and elbow dysplasia.

*Photo Courtesy
of Kalli McGilley*

Failing to notice early signs of potential issues can be detrimental, even fatal to your Schnoodle. As a fairly healthy breed, strange behavior in a Schnoodle is likely a sign of something that should be checked by your vet.

Prevention And Monitoring

Schnoodles may be cute when they are overweight, but an unhealthy habit of overfeeding can cause severe damage to his health. This is a breed that is already lovable, and you should never sacrifice your dog's health in the name of cuteness. Instead, take extra time to exercise with your dog; a habit which is healthier and more fun for both of you!

Checking your Schnoodle's weight is important and should be done at least once a quarter or twice a year. You and your vet should keep an eye on your dog's weight; being overweight puts a strain on your dog's back, legs, joints, and muscles. Obesity can also have adverse effects on your dog's heart, blood flow, and respiratory system.

Make sure to talk to your vet if you notice your Schnoodle has any problems related to obesity. Regular vet visits can help you address issues you may think are unimportant, but sometimes those symptoms are a sign of a future problem.

CHAPTER 17
The Aging Schnoodle

The average life expectancy of a Schnoodle is between ten and fifteen years depending on the Schnoodle's size (smaller dogs live longer). If you take loving care of your Schnoodle, you will enjoy more time with your buddy. Of course, it will never seem like it is enough time, but there is a lot you can do to extend your dog's life. A Schnoodle that is well-taken care of will live longer. This makes it all the more important to make sure your pup gets regular exercise and has a good diet.

At some point, you will notice your Schnoodle is slowing down. This usually happens between seven to ten years of age. (Again, this depends on the dog's size.) A dog may remain healthy his whole life, but as the years start to take their toll, his body may not be able to enjoy the same activities. The changes that are necessary as your dog ages will be based on your Schnoodle's specific needs.

The first signs of aging usually appear as a stiffness in his gait or heavy panting that begins early in your walk. If you see these changes, start to cut back on the long walks and go for shorter ones more often. Your Schnoodle may want to continue to be active, which calls for an adjustment in his activities but not a complete stop.

Be sure your pup doesn't overexert himself if he tries to remain active. Your Schnoodle may not want to accept the fact that things are changing; however, he will have no control over the changes.

There is a reason this period of time is called the Golden Years...you can relax and enjoy this time of your dog's life as well. You don't have to worry about him tearing up things because he's bored or becoming overexcited when seeing a squirrel during his walks. Instead, you can enjoy lazy evenings, peaceful weekends, and less-strenuous exercise. It's easy to make the senior years incredibly enjoyable for your Schnoodle and yourself by making the necessary adjustments.

Senior Care Challenges

Accommodations you should make for your senior Schnoodle include:
- Set water bowls in a couple of different places so your dog can reach them easily.
- Cover hard floor surfaces (such as tile, hardwood, and vinyl) with non-slip carpets or rugs.
- Use cushions and softer bedding for your Schnoodle to make things more comfortable. There are even bed warmers for dogs if your Schnoodle displays achy joints or muscles. You also need to make sure he isn't too warm, so this can be a fine balancing act.
- To improve his circulation, increase how often you brush your Schnoodle.
- Keep him inside in extreme heat or cold. An old canine cannot handle changes in temperature as well as he once did.
- Use stairs or ramps so the old pup doesn't have to do any jumping.
- Avoid moving furniture around in your home, particularly if your Schnoodle shows signs of problems with his eyesight or if he has dementia. A familiar home is more comforting and less stressful for your pet as he ages. If your Schnoodle isn't able to see as clearly as he once did, you should make sure his surroundings remain familiar to him, which will make it easier for him to move around without hurting himself.
- Consider organizing an area for your dog which allows him to avoid stairs, especially if climbing seems to bother him.
- Create a space with fewer distractions and noises where your Schnoodle can relax. Don't make your old friend feel isolated; instead, give him a place where he can get away from everyone if he needs to be alone.
- Be prepared to let your dog outside for restroom breaks more often.

Common Physical Disorders Related To Aging

Previous chapters address illnesses that are common in a Schnoodle. However, old age tends to bring a slew of ailments that are not particular to any one breed. Here are other things you will need to watch for (as well as talking to your vet about if they occur):

- Arthritis is probably the most common ailment in any dog breed, and the Schnoodle is no exception. If your dog is experiencing stiffness and pain after normal activities, discuss ways to help minimize his pain and discomfort.

- Gum disease is a common issue in older dogs as well, and you should continue brushing your dog's teeth on a regular basis as he ages. A regular check of your Schnoodle's teeth and gums can help ensure no problem develops.

- Loss of eyesight or blindness is relatively common in older dogs, just as it is in humans. Have your dog's vision checked at least once a year or more often if it is obvious his eyesight is failing.

- Kidney disease is a frequent problem in older dogs and one that you should watch for as your Schnoodle ages. If your canine drinks a lot of water and has accidents frequently, take him to the vet as soon as possible and have him checked for kidney disease.

- Although diabetes is usually thought of as a genetic condition, any Schnoodle can become diabetic if not fed and exercised properly. This is another reason why it's so important to be careful with your Schnoodle's diet and exercise levels.

Vet Visits

As your Schnoodle ages, slowing down and occasional pain will become obvious, just as it is in an older person. If your Schnoodle has a debilitating ailment or condition, you could discuss options for giving him a better quality of life. For example, wheelchairs are available if your Schnoodle shows problems with mobility.

The Importance Of Regular Vet Visits And What To Expect

Just as humans visit the doctor more often as they age, you'll need to take your dog to see your vet with greater frequency, too. The vet can make sure your Schnoodle stays active without overdoing it, and he can help alleviate unnecessary stress in your dog's life. If your canine has sustained an injury and hidden it from you, your vet is also more likely to detect the damage.

Based on your Schnoodle's changing personality and physical abilities, your vet might recommend changes to your dog's daily schedule and to his typical activities. For example, if your Schnoodle is panting more than before, it could be a sign of pain from stiffness. Your vet can help recommend the best way to keep your Schnoodle happy and active during the later years.

The following are the kinds of things to expect when you go to the vet:

- Your vet is going to talk about your dog's history even if you have visited every year. This talk is necessary to see how your dog's life has changed over time and to pinpoint when problems manifested themselves or got worse.
- Your vet will probably conduct a complete physical examination to assess your dog's current health.
- Depending on your dog's age and on his health, your vet may want to run some tests. The following are some of the most common tests for older dogs:
  - Arthropod-borne disease testing, which involves drawing blood and testing it for viral infections
  - Chemistry screening for kidney, liver, and sugar evaluation
  - Complete blood count
  - Fecal flotation, which involves mixing your dog's poop with a special liquid to test for worms and other parasites
  - Heartworm testing
  - Urinalysis, which tests your dog's urine to check the health of his kidneys and urinary system
- Routine wellness check, which the vet has been conducting on your dog for years.
- Any breed-specific tests for your aging Schnoodle.

Changes That Might Occur

Keep an eye out for different signs that your dog is slowing down. This will help you to know when to adjust the setup around your home and to reduce how much your old pup is exercising.

Appetite And Nutritional Requirements

With less exercise, your dog won't need as many calories as usual, which means you will need to adjust his diet. If you opted to feed your Schnoodle commercial dog food, make sure to change to a senior dog formula. Senior food is designed for the changing dietary needs of older dogs by including fewer calories and adding more nutrients,

If you prepare dog food at home, talk to your vet and research how best to reduce calories without sacrificing taste. Your canine is going to need less fat in his diet, so you should make healthier food choices while still considering the taste. These dietary changes will certainly be different from the puppy and active adult foods you fed your Schnoodle in the past.

Exercise

It's up to you to adjust your dog's schedule and to keep him less active yet happy. Shorter and more frequent walks should take care of your Schnoodle's exercise needs, as well as helping to break up your day a little more.

Your dog will enjoy napping as much as walking, especially if he gets to cuddle with you. Sleeping beside you while you watch television or as you nap is pretty much all it takes to make your older Schnoodle content!

You may notice your Schnoodle spends more time sniffing during walks, which could be a sign that your dog is tiring. If he is walking slower, looking up at you, and flopping down, that could be his way of letting you know it's time to return home. If your canine can no longer manage long walks, make them shorter and more often. You could also spend more time romping around your yard or at home with your buddy.

Aging And The Senses

Just like people, dogs' senses weaken as they get older. They won't hear things as well as they used to, they won't see things as clearly, and their sense of smell will weaken.

The following are some of the signs your dog is losing at least one of his senses:

- It becomes easy to surprise or startle your dog. You need to be careful because this can make your Schnoodle aggressive, which is a scary prospect even in old age.

- Your dog may seem to ignore you or is less responsive when you issue a command.

- Cloudy eyes may be a sign of sight loss, though it does not mean your dog is blind.

If your aging dog seems to "behave badly", it is a sign that he is aging, not that he wants to rebel. Do not punish your older dog.

Adjust your schedule to meet your dog's changing

CELEBRITY SCHNOODLES

The World's Oldest Schnoodle ★★★★

According to Guinness World Records, the oldest recorded Schnoodle lived for twenty years and one hundred and fifty-four days. He lived in the United States, and his name was Winston Rha. Winston was born on December 12, 1992, and died on May 15, 2013.

abilities. Adjust his water bowl's height, refrain from rearranging rooms, and pet your dog more often. Make sure his bed is fluffy or get him a new, more comfortable bed. Put the bed on the floor if it was previously kept on furniture. Your dog is probably nervous about losing his abilities, so it is up to you to comfort him.

Keeping Your Senior Dog Mentally Active

Just because your older Schnoodle can't walk as far as he used to, doesn't mean his brain is weaker, too. As long as your Schnoodle performs all of the basic commands, you can teach him all kinds of new, low-impact tricks.

At this point, training could be easier because your Schnoodle has learned to focus better, and he'll be happy to have something he can still do with you. New toys are another fun way to help keep your dog's mind active. Be careful the toys aren't too rough on your dog's jaw and teeth. There are also food balls, puzzles, and other games that focus on cognitive abilities... and games such as hide and seek will still be very much appreciated!

Some senior dogs suffer from Cognitive Dysfunction (CCD) Syndrome, a type of dementia. It is estimated that 85% of all cases of dementia in dogs go undiagnosed because of how difficult it is to pinpoint the problem. It manifests itself more as a problem of temperament than of cognitive ability.

If your dog begins to act differently, you should take him to the vet to see if he has CCD. While there really isn't any treatment for this problem, your vet can recommend things that will help your dog focus. An action such as rearranging the furniture is strongly discouraged because your dog relies on the familiarity of his surroundings. Being accustomed to the arrangement will make your dog comfortable and will reduce his stress. Mental stimulation at this time of your Schnoodle's life is a still a must. Not only will keeping his mind active fight CCD, but it will also keep him healthy whether he exhibits signs of dementia or not.

Advantages To The Senior Years

The last years of your Schnoodle's life can be just as enjoyable (if not more so) than the earlier stages since your dog has mellowed over time. All those high-energy activities will give way to relaxing and enjoying time with you, which can be a peaceful and comforting respite. Yet, you must remember to include mild activities during the day, so your dog does not become too complacent. Your Schnoodle's newfound love of resting and simply taking it easy can be addictive!

Your Schnoodle will continue to be a loving companion, interacting with you at every opportunity – that does not change with age. However, your canine's limitations should dictate interactions and activities. If you are busy, make sure you schedule time with your Schnoodle to do things that are within those limitations. It is just as easy to make an older Schnoodle happy as it is to make a young dog happy!

Preparing To Say Goodbye

No pet parent wants to think about this last step, but as you watch your Schnoodle slow down, you will know when your time with your sweet pup is coming to an end. Some dogs can continue to live for years after they begin to slow down, but many dogs don't make it more than a year or two. Sometimes dogs will lose their interest in eating, will have a stroke, or another problem will arise without warning. Eventually, it will be time to say goodbye, whether at home or at the vet's office. You need to be prepared and that is exactly why you should be making the most of these last few years.

Talk to your family about how you should care for your dog over the last few years or months of his life. Many dogs will be perfectly happy continuing life as usual, despite their limited abilities. Some may begin to have problems controlling their bowel movements, while others may have problems getting up from a prone position. There are solutions to all of these problems. Always remember quality of life should be your primary concern. Since your dog cannot tell you how he feels, you must take cues from your dog. If your dog still seems happy, there is no reason to have him euthanized.

At this stage, your dog is probably happy just sleeping near you for eighteen hours a day. This is perfectly fine as long as he still gets excited about walking, eating, and being petted. The purpose of euthanasia is to reduce suffering, not to make things more convenient for yourself. This is what makes the decision so difficult, but your dog's behavior should be a fairly good indicator of how he is feeling. Here are some other things to watch when evaluating your dog's quality of life:

- Appetite
- Drinking
- Urinating and defecation
- Pain (noted by excessive panting)
- Stress levels
- Desire to be active or with family (If your dog wants to be alone most of the time, this is usually a sign he is trying to be alone for the end of his life.)

Talk to your vet if your dog has a serious illness to determine the best path forward. They can provide the best information on the quality of your dog's life and how long your dog is likely to live with his disease or ailment.

If your dog gets to the point where he is no longer happy, he can't move around, or he has a fatal illness, it is probably time to say goodbye. This is a decision that should be made as a family, always putting the dog's needs and quality of life first. If you decide it is time to say goodbye, determine who will be present at the end.

If you have decided to euthanize your dog, you can make his last few minutes calming and peaceful by feeding your dog the things he couldn't eat before. Things like chocolate and grapes can put a smile on his face for his remaining time in your life.

You can also have your dog euthanized at home. If you decide to request a vet to come to your home, be prepared for additional charges for the home visit. You also need to determine where you want your dog to be, whether inside or outside, and in which room if you decide to do it inside.

Make sure at least one person he knows well is present, so your dog is not alone during the last few minutes of his life. You don't want your dog to die surrounded by strangers. The process is fairly peaceful, but your dog will probably be a little stressed. He will pass within a few minutes of the injection but continue to talk to him as his brain will continue to work even after his eyes close.

Once your dog is gone, you need to determine what to do with the body:

- Cremation is one of the most common ways of taking care of the body. You can request an urn or ask for a container for his ashes so you can scatter your dog's ashes over his favorite places. Make sure you don't spread his ashes in places where this action is not permitted. Private cremation is more expensive than communal cremation, but it means the only ashes you receive are from your dog. Communal cremation occurs when several pets are cremated together.

- Burial is the easiest method after your dog is euthanized and can be performed at your home. However, you need to check local regulations to be sure burying your dog on your property is legal. You also need to consider the soil; if your yard is rocky or sandy, that will create problems when trying to bury your pet. Also, don't bury your pet in a spot that is near a well that people use as a drinking source or if it is near wetlands or waterways. Your dog's body can contaminate the water as it decays. You can also look into a pet cemetery if there is one in your area.

Grief And Healing

Dogs become members of our families, so their passing can be incredibly difficult. People go through all of the same emotions and feelings of loss with a dog as they do with close friends and family. The absence of your dog's presence in your life is jarring, especially with such a loving, loyal dog like the Schnoodle. It will feel weird not to have that presence by your side as you move around your home, and it will be a constant reminder of your loss. In the beginning, you and your family will probably feel considerable grief. Saying goodbye will be extremely difficult, so taking a couple of days off work is not a bad idea. While some people might say your Schnoodle was "just a dog", you know better; it is okay to feel the pain and to grieve like you would for any lost loved one.

Losing your Schnoodle is also going to create a substantial change in your schedule. It will likely take a while to become accustomed to the shift in your day-to-day life. Fight the urge to go out and get a new dog because you almost certainly will not be ready yet.

Everyone grieves differently so allow yourself to grieve in a way that is healthy for you. Everyone in your family will feel the loss differently, too, so let them do the same. Some people don't require much time, while others can feel the loss for months. There is no timetable, so don't try to force it on yourself or on any member of your family.

Talk about how you would like to remember your pup. You can have a memorial for your lost pet, tell stories, or plant a tree in your dog's memory.

Try to return to your normal routine as much as possible if you have other pets. This can be both painful and helpful as your other pets will still need you just as much as when your Schnoodle was alive. This is especially true of other dogs that have also lost their companion.

If you find grief is hindering your ability to function normally, seek professional help. If needed, you can search online to find support groups in your area to help you and your family, especially if this was your first dog. Sometimes it helps to talk about the loss so that you can begin to heal.

Made in the USA
Las Vegas, NV
17 January 2022

41623704R00094